CRUCIFIED HEROES

The Films of Sam Peckinpah

CRUCIFIED HEROES

The Films of Sam Peckinpah

TERENCE BUTLER

GORDON FRASER · LONDON 1979

First published 1979 by
The Gordon Fraser Gallery Ltd., London and Bedford

ISBN 0 86092 008 9 hardcover
ISBN 0 86092 009 7 softcover

Text set in 'Monotype' Plantin series 110 and printed by
The Roundwood Press, Kineton, Warwick
Illustrations printed by The Stellar Press, Hatfield, Hertfordshire
Made and printed in Great Britain

CONTENTS

ACKNOWLEDGEMENTS

I am indebted to: Robin Wood, for providing me with some of the initial stimulus to write the book; Richard Dacre, for typing out the manuscript; Anthony Budd of Granada, for help with research; Mike Wallington, for editing the manuscript; Jack 'Kamakaze' Shotton, for special help; Charles Harmel-Rubinstein of the Other Cinema, for ideological guidance; and Sam Peckinpah, for his easy-going courtesy to me and, more importantly, for persevering to make his films.

Stills by courtesy of the Stills Library of the National Film Archive (London), Columbia-Warner, EMI, Fox-Rank, MGM, Scotia Barber, United Artists.

This book is dedicated to the memory of Roman Voelpel, who had no luck right up to the end, and who had a lot of friends.

In the desert
I saw a creature, naked, bestial,
Who, squatting upon the ground,
Held his heart in his hands
And ate of it.
I said, 'Is it good, friend?'
'It is bitter, bitter,' he answered.
'But I like it
Because it is bitter,
And because it is my heart.'

Stephen Crane, *Black Riders* III

To view Sam Peckinpah's work as a whole is to notice some changes in technique and execution. Yet, ever subjected to revision and deepening, the same themes recur from film to film. The aim of this book is to define the manner in which these themes are developed and to examine how they constitute a commentary on American society.

Although far from conventional genre pictures, most of Peckinpah's movies have been Westerns. So as good a point as any to begin a study of his work is from the point of view of the Western.

Recent genre criticism has been surprisingly neutral in the attitudes it has adopted. Reacting against the snobbishness that in the past had held American genre cinema in such low esteem, genre critics have tended to be over-reverential to genre conventions. Value has often been placed on a director's work simply because the director inflects genre conventions in an original way. Little attempt has been made to view the strategies behind such inflections in a political light.

Like any other genre of American cinema, the Western has been produced and developed through a strange convergence of national spirit, business enterprise and the personal visions of individuals, so any definition of it must inevitably be loose. Although this book makes no claim to present a fixed definition of what constitutes the Western, it does set out to examine certain themes that are peculiar to the Western and related areas of American cinema. One of the things that the Western has most consistently achieved has been to delineate the workings of an oppressively patriarchal society, a world so haunted by a nightmare figure of the father that individual emotional development can only be crippled. Such concerns, however, have often been presented in a fallacious manner. Patriotic fervour, a naïve faith in the value of social change and similar attitudes have served as blinds to the genre's Gothic preoccupations.

The main impulse behind Peckinpah's cinema is a need to focus on an area of pain that so much American cinema seeks to conceal. To appreciate Peckinpah's work is to acknowledge that the psychopath is truly a hero of the American cinema, that the often covert existence of the psychopath's mentality behind so many movies has all along been an outcry against the intolerable burden of certain social constraints. Operating on a more balanced level than Peckinpah, directors as diverse as John Huston, Francis Ford Coppola and Robert Rossen have reached similar conclusions on the repressive force of power. Yet what makes Peckinpah so unique is the way he chooses to make his statement by operating so rigorously through the conventions of genre cinema. Peckinpah has none of the detachment towards genre conventions so often shown recently by directors of so-called 'anti-Westerns'; his relationship to the Western is a love-hate one. If Peckinpah responds to the Western's view of the frontier as something vital, he rejects its view of Anglo-Saxon society as a civilizing force. Peckinpah's resolve to make Westerns, therefore, comes as an enraged acknowledgement of a particular cultural fatedness.

Miller, the 'psycho' of *The Killer Elite*, is at one point called 'the patron poet of the manic depressives': this term could well be applied to Peckinpah himself. The director's hard-drinking and wild social life have received much publicity, as has the 'creative paranoia' with which he goes about the job of making movies. 'A director has to deal with a whole world absolutely teeming with mediocrities, jackals, hangers-on and just plain killers', Peckinpah has said of his occupation. 'The attrition is terrific. It can kill you. The saying is that they can kill you but not eat you. That's nonsense. I've had them eating on me while I was still walking around.' It seems that the scorpions writhing amid killer ants in the opening of *The Wild Bunch* could also stand as an image for the director's own torment.

Peckinpah's cinema is the cinema of a mind at the end of its tether. Inevitably its emotional force is not always agreeable. But even its instances of misogyny have value in that they expose the consequences of certain forms of repression. Peckinpah cares only about the inner self; he cannot bring himself to present in a socially acceptable manner any of the violent emotions he feels. It is from this that his cinema derives a Nietzschean drive to the extremes of immediate transcendence.

Some objections could be made about the validity of Peckinpah's themes. It could be argued that Peckinpah is too obsessed with America's past hang-ups, that for all the contemporary allusions of his Westerns (the pre-Tea Dome Scandal era of *Pat Garrett and Billy the Kid* is meant to have parallels with Watergate) or the contemporary settings of his other action movies (*The Getaway* or *The Killer Elite*), it is the oppressively patriarchal world of the Western and America's past with which Peckinpah deals. Yet even if this is true, it does not affect the relative validity of the judgements he makes on the social configurations he describes. A frequent objection to his work is that he cannot present women as individuals; and while this is not totally true (both *The Ballad of Cable Hogue* and *The Getaway* have strong female protagonists), many of his women are shadowy figures. Yet it seems to me that Peckinpah made an implicit acknowledgement of his limitation by choosing to make Westerns, the kind of cultural dispositions that dominate the genre being primarily those open to the male psyche.

Some commentators on the American cinema claim that recent American movies reflect a breakdown in American values and general loss of faith. Peckinpah in particular has been accused of nihilism. Yet it is surely not so much that values have broken down but that the values were sick and twisted in the first place. To counter accusations of nihilism made against Peckinpah, the first part of this book examines his work in relation to pre-existing attitudes in American cinema and literature. A number of American writers are mentioned not because Peckinpah claims to have read them but because they prefigure the director – in their work, respect for the freedom of the frontier mingles with an isolative and introspective outlook. In terms of American cinema prior to Peckinpah, I prefer to examine how other directors have tackled similar themes to Peckinpah than simply to delineate the contours of genre.

The second section of this book examines Peckinpah's movies individually. The aim here is less to defend their formal qualities than to delineate how Peckinpah's themes and preoccupations are worked out. In movies by directors like John Ford and Howard Hawks, I find the formal qualities interesting but the ideological concerns deviously handled. With Peckinpah, on the other hand, it is the ruthless honesty with which he pursues his themes that I find so impressive. To *Straw Dogs*, his movies are at their most formally achieved. Both *Junior Bonner* and *The Getaway*, despite great pieces, contain brief instances of clumsy direction, and in *Pat Garrett and Billy the Kid* and *Bring Me the Head of Alfredo Garcia* whole scenes are shabbily shot. Yet *Alfredo Garcia* has a mesmerizing power; even a strange non-performance from Isela Vega, its leading lady, seems to work for the movie. With Warren Oates made up to look like Peckinpah, we have one of the director's most forceful attempts to confront the forces that oppress him: *Alfredo Garcia* has the strange distinction of being the worst directed of great American movies. *The Killer Elite*, smoothly directed and with good dialogue delivery (often extraordinary in scenes involving Gig Young and Arthur Hill), signifies a return to formal coherence, while *Cross of Iron*, a vast panorama of chaotic action, probably has more individual shots than any other Peckinpah movie and repeatedly gives the impression of hanging together *just*. It is difficult to see how far Peckinpah can go from here; a total fragmentation of vision seems not yet beyond the director's disproportionate temperament.

PECKINPAH, THE WESTERN AND AMERICAN GOTHIC

> 'If absence from repression is the archetype of freedom, then civilization is the struggle against freedom.'
>
> Herbert Marcuse, *Eros and Civilization*

Many American writers have resented the civilization that spread westwards from the east across their continent. Mark Twain and Stephen Crane saw the frontier as the repository of a unique vitality and spontaneity. 'Culture . . .,' Crane wrote, 'is a comprehension of the man at one's shoulder. It has nothing to do with an adoration of effete jugs and old kettles. The latter is merely an amusement and we live for amusement in the east. Damn the east! I fell in love with the straight out-and-out, sometimes hideous, often braggart westerners because I thought them to be the truer men.' Other writers saw the frontier in terms of an awe-inspiring violence. Herman Melville compared his Moby Dick to 'the White Steed of the Prairies' which brings to mind 'the glories of primeval times when Adam walked majestic as a god'. In the writings of Jack London a commitment to the frontier is bound up with a delight in atavism, in the ability of the primitive self to shred the constraints of civilization. London's *White Fang,* which deals with a wolf cub's removal from the wild and adoption by an eastern family, is characterized by a growing sense of unresolved tension, while in *The Call of the Wild,* about a dog's movement in the reverse direction, from the east to the life of a beast in the wild, the narrative moves forward to a celebration of instinct and frenzy. London's description of his canine hero's first real awareness of the promptings of the savage animal within him is one of the most beautiful passages in American literature:

'There is an ecstasy that makes the summit of life, and beyond which life cannot rise. And such is the paradox of living, this ecstasy comes when one is most alive, and it comes as a complete forgetfulness that one is alive. This ecstasy, this forgetfulness of living, comes to the artist caught up and out of himself in a sheet of flame; it comes to the soldier, war-mad on a stricken field and refusing quarter; and it came to Buck, leading the pack, sounding the old wolf cry, straining after the food that was alive and that fled swiftly before him through the moonlight. He was sounding the deeps of his nature, and of the parts of his nature that were deeper than he, going back into the womb of Time. He was mastered by the sheer surging of life, the tidal wave of being, the perfect joy of each separate muscle, joint, and sinew in that it was everything that was not death, that it was aglow and rampant, expressing itself in movement, flying exultantly under the stars and over the face of dead matter that did not move.'

The writer generally cited as the most direct precursor of the Western is James Fenimore Cooper, who created the character of Leatherstocking, the denizen of the wilderness who shuns civilized society and yet feels compelled to be its harbinger. Yet Cooper, a member of the New England gentry, proved incapable of examining the contradictions inherent in his hero. It is perhaps fitting that such a conservative should be considered the father of the Western. As we might expect from a form of popular entertainment, the Western, at least as it largely was until the 'sixties, has sought to make the provocative officially acceptable and thus has tended to bastardize the commitment to the frontier evinced by America's best writers; in many respects, the Western has sought to convince its audience that there was nothing at all odious about the impact of Anglo-Saxon society upon the frontier. The traditional Western hero (if we may call him this) would claim to love the open spaces and wear the apparel of the frontier, but his morality, as with Cooper's Leatherstocking, came in many ways from the east. He would often act with a moral sense divorced from spontaneity and instinct, and his behaviour, if rough and ready, was never ungentlemanly enough to scandalize the ladies. In taking up arms against Indians and badmen, he would take it upon himself to climinate the wildness so beloved of Stephen Crane and Jack London. Such conduct is a kind of puritanism. Indeed, this hero's shunning of society often seems more an emanation of New England protestantism than an indication of any oneness with nature; to discover this we have only to compare his isolation to that urged by Emerson in his protestantism-influenced essay 'On Self-Reliance'. Appropriately a number of Westerns, among them John Ford's *The Searchers* and Raoul Walsh's *The Lawless Breed,* have used a demented preacher as a mirror image of the hero.

However, if puritanism remained the dominant ideology of the Western until the 'sixties, a genuine commitment to the frontier often emerged covertly. Cecil B.DeMille, with his Westerns and backwoods dramas, *The Plainsman, Union Pacific, Northwest Mounted Police* and *The Unconquered,* made the most concerted attempt to present frontier and civilization as an integrated whole, and as a bizarre consequence of this he exposes the two as actually polarized. DeMille's heroes not only hold the community in awe, but also social change and industrial progress. Their final triumph becomes the triumph of a nation: 'And so this great nation is united by a wedding ring of iron,' DeMille tells us at the end of *Union Pacific,* thus linking the blossoming love of his hero and heroine with the success of the railroad. DeMille continually seeks to show that man is inveterately anarchic and that repressive controls, like those which come through Church and Army, are necessary. In *Northwest Mounted Police,* for instance, Indians revolt not because of an injustice done towards them but out of a compulsion to wreak havoc: the very sight of a gatling-gun fills them with subversive delight. But DeMille always defeats himself: his heroes remain too individualistic to adapt to the order they help create; his villains and *femmes fatales* are often the most attractive characters in his movies; and his intuitive response to the majesty of the wilderness always undercuts the claims he puts for civilization. Ultimately, what DeMille dramatizes is a conflict between the dead tameness of civilization and the elemental forces.

The Western has often viewed women in terms of sexual disgust. As American society evolved, its puritanism dulled and sexuality, instead of being condemned, was totally ignored; Leslie Fiedler in *Love and Death in the American Novel* sees this shift in terms of a father-centred protestantism giving way to what he calls 'the Sentimental Love Religion, which simultaneously disowns sex and glorifies woman'. Women in the frontier were called upon to contribute the standards of conduct and spiritual values without which the community would break down, and they became increasingly inflexible in the manner they carried this out. In general it is at its most debased (particularly in silent and 'B' Westerns) that this view of woman has been extolled. The woman is often a demure creature who wears the apparel of the east, she has little or no understanding of the Western hero and yet it is on her terms that he must gauge his moral worthiness. Robert Warshow perceptively saw her relationship to the hero as constituting a clash between east and west. Set alongside the demure heroine, though never a serious threat to her sovereignty, is the saloon girl. Since the saloon girl is practical and sexually frank, she is a more suitable companion for the Western hero. Yet we see in her the operation of the old Calvinist equation of sexuality and sin; saloon girl is, after all, just a euphemism for prostitute. So she often ends up dying nobly to atone for her sinful ways. Another stereotype is the Indian girl: she has mostly figured in the more prestigious Western productions, having never really taken hold in the genre until the 'fifties when the 'Indian Western' became fashionable. Yet if her appearance in the genre appears somewhat artificial in relation to that of the demure heroine and saloon girl, she is similarly a product of pre-existing attitudes to women. In one respect she takes us back to Longfellow: recalling his depiction of his Indian heroine in *The Song of Hiawatha,* directors of diverse sensibilities have chosen to associate the Indian girl with rivers, streams and Edenic naturalness. The Indian girl also recalls the Polynesian girls of Herman Melville's *Typee:* like them, she is free from all notions of Anglo-Saxon propriety and is usually an uncomplicated conquest for the hero. She can be passive and submissive to the point of being almost a nonentity, as in Howard Hawks' *The Big Sky*. Like the saloon girl, the Indian girl often ends up dying. Her death can be accompanied by nostalgia and regret, as if signifying an expulsion from paradise for the Western hero (Delmer Daves' *Broken Arrow,* William Wellman's *Across the Wide Missouri)*. Ralph Nelson's fairly recent *The Wrath of God* seeks to exorcise an old stereotype instead of adopting a more enlightened attitude towards women; its Indian girl heroine is dumb (literally) and to many of the movie's male characters only a target for rape.

America's elevation of the mother to a dominant position within its culture was bound up with its split from Europe, whom it felt compelled to reject as its symbolic father. Yet this did not mean that America became a matriarchal society: what happened was that the mother assumed an authoritarian role within a patriarchal framework. It is largely this transition that Leslie Fiedler in *Love and Death in the American Novel* blames for the disowning of sex that characterizes the genesis of American literature. For Fiedler, American literature's Gothic obsessions and its eager approval of toughness reflect the nation's anxieties about sex. Fiedler, like a number of other critics, studies *Moby Dick* in terms of how certain tensions in the American psyche seek catharsis: in terms of the repressive cultural attitudes of the time, the mad Captain Ahab's pursuit of the White Whale takes on a particular significance, the whale bearing for Ahab the imagos of his cultural parentage, a wrathful father and a cold mother.

In American cinema, Ahab-like revolt can be found most often in a clandestine form, ostensibly noble intentions in a hero capable of revealing themselves as shot through with aggression and hostility. *Tol'able David,* Henry King's rural drama, provides a good example of how in American cinema an approval of toughness can merge with a sentimentalization of filial piety to mask an Oedipal guilt. *Tol'able David* enjoyed an enormous popular appeal when it first appeared; it tells the story of a clean-living young man who wins the approval of his mother by killing a group of escaped convicts who have injured his brother and hastened the death of his ailing father. On a subliminal level, beneath its sentimentality, the movie emerges as a study of a young man burdened by patriarchal authority. David, it can be argued, feels compelled to define himself through violence as the father of the family because of anxieties about doing so sexually; thus, in killing the convicts, he is killing the transgressor in himself to appease the ghost of his father. In this light the convicts also come to function as socially acceptable targets for an aggression in David that springs from actual resentment of both paternal imperiousness and maternal aloofness.

Although *Tol'able David* is not a Western, its subliminal themes are refracted through the Western. The characteristic ambivalence of the traditional Western hero recalls the psychology of *Tol'able David;* boundless tolerance of female chastity and eruptive violence against the community's enemies are key characteristics of the screen *personae* of many of the actors who have come to be associated with the Western. The American approval of toughness springs only partly from the association of an ideal of unsullied manliness with the frontier; it also arises from a compulsion to endorse butch behaviour so as to conceal the ravages that an oppressive patriarchy has effected on the male psyche. Often it is bound up with the coercion of a female sensibility. Recalling Cooper's Leatherstocking tales, a predominant relationship in the Western is the 'buddy love' friendship of two men, where one partner, the movie's hero, plays an aggressively masculine role and the other a passive, even wifely one. Anthony Mann's *Winchester '73*, John Ford's *The Searchers*, Charles Marquis Warren's *Arrowhead* are major Westerns that contain examples of this kind of relationship. In the last named of these the wife figure dies a 'Saint Sebastian' death peppered with Indian arrows, the essential masochism of his role made apparent.

In the Western heterosexual union is always problematical because there can be no easy reconciliation between the poles of violence and woman. A frequent reconciliation of the poles – and one which is essentially unsatisfactory – is for the hero to have loved a woman 'once' and thus be able to pursue his career of violence, sustained by a sentimentalized image of woman. Perhaps underlying all the female stereotypes in the Western is just one type – a virago, who presents men with the eternal challenge of demonstrating their virility. A semi-convention of the genre until recently was that the gun was not to be brandished in the presence of woman. Both George Stevens' *Shane* and Tom Gries' *Will Penny* derive a good deal of their emotional intensity from the manner in which they have for heroines married women who are desired by the hero and who place a strict emphasis on the taboo against the gun: in both cases the drama is resolved by the hero choosing the gun to woman; he abandons his beloved to discharge his violence against socially hostile forces and then he rides away. The particular humanism of Nicholas Ray's *Johnny Guitar* derives from the way it rejects the taboo against the gun. Seeing Vienna only as a woman he loved 'once', Johnny returns to her as a gunfighter no longer. Eventually he brandishes his gun again against social elements threatening their relationship, thus redeeming her from a virago-like role.

More often in the Western, however, there is no way of renouncing violence through heterosexual union: usually woman is but the arbiter of an Oedipal pain, a mother figure for whom the price of loving is punishment. Jerry Thorpe's *The Day of The Evil Gun* is a Western that shows how the Western hero's career of violence can lead to a destiny of pain. The movie concerns a gunfighter who returns home to find that his wife and children have been abducted by Indians. The gunfighter sets out to rescue them, accompanied by another man who had planned to marry his wife. As the journey progresses, this would-be husband becomes increasingly obsessed by violence, and when the wife and children are rescued, there remains between the two men an antagonism to be resolved. The gunfighter gives his gun to a storekeeper in exchange for clothes for his wife and is wounded in the leg by his demented companion, the storekeeper using his gun to kill the attacker. If the gunfighter no longer needs vengefully to pursue a career of violence, the movie's conclusion is far from a happy one: the last image is not of the gunfighter reunited with his wife, but kneeling wounded in the street, the pain he bears seeming to exclude him from her forever.

The director the general public perhaps most readily associates with the Western is John Ford. Not just in his Westerns but throughout his movies, Ford presents sex and violence as inextricably linked, although he never proves able to explore fully the social implications of such a link. The *Cahiers du Cinéma* article on Ford's *Young Mr Lincoln,* reading against the populist sentimentality of the movie, sees Lincoln's compulsion to enforce law and order as a consequence of the prohibition of incest: the article places emphasis on the negligible part played by fathers in the movie and on the dominance of the mother of the two men Lincoln defends for murder, a woman who reminds him of his own mother.

Of all Ford's Westerns, *The Searchers* is the one that most openly tackles the link between sex and violence. In it John Wayne plays Ethan Edwards, a man who secretly yearns for his brother's wife. When the brother's homestead is massacred and the brother's wife ravished before being killed, Ethan sets off in pursuit of the Indians who were responsible, a band of Apache led by a chief called Scar. Ethan thus becomes a kind of Tol'able David. Ethan's growing obsession with killing Scar, whom he seems to feel is personally responsible for the ravishing of his brother's wife, springs from a need to destroy what he unconsciously fears as the transgressor in himself. The same terror at his phallic self also makes Ethan feel compelled to kill his brother's only surviving daughter, who has been abducted by Scar to live as his daughter; to Ethan's mind, the child has become linked with the idea of incest. At the same time Scar appears as a target for an aggression in Ethan that has its origins largely in misogyny and a resentment for authority. Ford, however, never criticizes the taboo system that has made Ethan what he is; *The Searchers* ends as, with Scar's village overrun, Ethan returns his brother's daughter to white society and rides mutely away.

Not all of Ford's Westerns attain the pessimism of *The Searchers,* but even those that fail in this indicate the manner in which civilization may finally prove corrosive. *My Darling Clementine,* made in 1946, ten years before *The Searchers,* is Ford both at his most conservative and anarchic. It is worth discussing here because Peckinpah regards it as one of his favourite movies and its contradictions have deeply influenced his work. In the relationship of Clementine, Wyatt Earp and Doc Holliday we find a *motif* that runs through the American cinema and goes back to the Leatherstocking tales via Jack London's *The Sea Wolf:* that of a man torn between the socializing influence of woman and the seeming freedom of male friendships. Viewed in terms of this *motif, My Darling Clementine* suggests that homosexual obsessions in the Western are a reflection of cultural sterility. Ford wants his audience to take the relationship between Wyatt Earp and Clementine seriously because, like DeMille in *Union Pacific,* he sees heterosexual union as making possible his hero's absorption into the grand evolution of America. Yet the union must be one of the least amorous courtships in the history of American cinema. Clementine is the demure heroine as cardboard cut-out: in fact, she derives her identity as a character almost exclusively from her eastern clothes. Earp's response to her appears prompted more by a sense of social obligation than any amorous inclination. This is particularly apparent in the scene where on a Sunday morning he leads her to a half-built church to the strains of 'Gather at the river', Ford desperately injecting patriotic sentiment to conceal a lack of substance in their relationship. Leslie Fiedler sees Fenimore Cooper's Leatherstocking drawn to Chingachgook, his redskin buddy, because the Indian embodies 'whatever has been starved to death in the American psyche': and, underlying the narcissistic 'buddy love', there is something similar about Wyatt Earp's relationship to Doc Holliday; for if, unlike Leatherstocking's Indian comrade, Holliday is sick and ailing, he can nevertheless lay claim to a biological integrity through the vitality of his violent outbursts. Thus, it is as if in his affection for Holliday Earp is unconsciously attempting a doomed rekindling of a vitality in himself destroyed by the values Clementine embodies. Earp's mistaken suspicion that Holliday is the murderer of his brother seems partly the result of fears he has about himself as a threat to the community. Holliday behaves like the Hyde to Earp's Jekyll. He has no desires on the movie's nominal heroine; Clementine is actually an ex-girlfriend of his and now he can feel only revulsion for her and what she stands for. His recitation of part of the most famous Hamlet soliloquy suggests his fascination with death and his knight-errantist demise in the gunfight at the O.K. Corral, avenging the death of his prostitute-girlfriend, has the quality of a suicidal gesture that runs against a puritan notion of redemption also implicit in it. 'Crashing out', an American slang expression for prison break, was a phrase coined by Raoul Walsh in his *High Sierra* to describe the moment when a man goes under by squaring off against forces both within and without himself; and if Holliday does not die by going up against a police-force as a number of Walsh's heroes do, his death is nevertheless a denial of a repressive law. In the gunfight, Earp sees the lawless Clantons as forces that must be wiped out if public decency is to be preserved, but since Holliday goes up against them because one of them has killed the woman he tried to love, he implicitly confronts them as a mirror image of the subtle tyranny of Earp's law enforcement. If Earp ends as the survivor, he is by no means a triumphant one, for Holliday's death serves as a reminder of just how much Earp must compromise to remain part of the community.

If we view objectively the manner in which Ford presents the development of civilization, we discover this development to be characterized by repression and atrophy. We find a compulsion to block heterosexual desire. This blocking produces a violence that seeks to eliminate what sparks of Eros remain. The instruments of this violence become estranged and finally discarded by society, resulting in the establishment of a sterile culture. A father figure is often associated with sexual renunciation in Ford's Westerns: in *Fort Apache* a mad colonel from the east leads a detachment of cavalry to their deaths and away from the women who love them; while in *Rio Grande* John Wayne's cavalry captain is repeatedly ordered on dangerous missions away from his wife by a commander whom Ford depicts as a devil figure. Curiously, while in his later work Ford showed increasing dismay at the erosion of the frontier, he endorsed all the more fervently the kind of repressions that effected this: in *The Man Who Shot Liberty Valance* (1962), for instance, Wayne's natural aristocrat of a rancher mutely accepts that he must lose the woman he loves to a lawyer from the east, another Fordian son accepting the law. Yet in *Two Rode Together* (1961) Ford managed to confront the obverse of his mother worship when in something approaching a sexual gesture a white boy rescued from Indians kills the white woman claiming to be his mother and then is rapidly lynched in accordance with the dictates of the community's law.

Henry Hathaway and Howard Hawks are two other directors who, like Ford and DeMille, have to some degree endorsed the colonization of the West as a movement towards repression. Hathaway's often celibate heroes usually feel compelled to become the arbiters of patriarchal authority: in *True Grit* this happens by the hero becoming the avenger for a wronged family and in *The Sons of Katie Elder* and *Nevada Smith* by setting out to revenge wrongs done to his own family. Like Ford, Hathaway never properly reflects on the mechanism of the violence he depicts. *The Shepherd of the Hills,* which has John Wayne out to kill his own father for wronging his mother, is Hathaway's most openly Oedipal Western, but it is spoiled by a false reconciliation between father and son. Hawks' Westerns, particularly *Rio Bravo, El Dorado* and *Rio Lobo,* reveals the protestantism of the Western at its worst. Hawks deviously depicts women as a threat to his heroes' emotional stability, yet it is surely an obsession with demonstrating manliness that really fouls up such heroes. As with *Johnny Guitar,* Hawks' Westerns provide a notable exception to the taboo against the gun. Hawks' heroes always make a point of brandishing their guns before women, yet this does not suggest an assuming of sexual responsibility as in the Ray film. Here the gun provides a pretext for the heroes not to become involved with women, serving as an indication to the women that the heroes have urgent, manly business on hand. Hawks' heroes are preoccupied with living up to a harsh professional code of being 'good enough' and this is usually bound up with enforcing the law: a man only has a right to respect if he can always pull himself together and do his job. Predictably the female is suppressed in Hawks' Westerns, women not only always relegated to the periphery of the action but the androgyny of Hawks' young guns ruthlessly subordinated to John Wayne's butch *persona.* Yet for all this Hawks' male groups exude at times an appealing vitality.

Other directors have made more discerning commentaries on the Western's preoccupations. Budd Boetticher's Westerns (e.g. *The Tall T, Ride Lonesome)* present a bleak world where solipsism has as many limitations as advantages and death is the final proof of the isolation of living in a man's world. On the other hand, Delmer Daves at his best was able to imbue the Western with a mysterious gentleness: hence in *3.10 to Yuma* the familial pressures that compel a farmer to enforce the law are countered by the tender impact a saloon girl's love has on an outlaw. William Wellman's Westerns are in many ways a rebuke against the necessity of a man's world. In *The Robin Hood of El Dorado, Buffalo Bill* and *Across the Wide Missouri,* the heroes are plunged into permanent disorientation by the deaths of the women they love, and both *The Ox-Bow Incident* and *Yellow Sky* have bar-room scenes where bored and dissatisfied drifters look longingly at paintings of women. Through the study of a lynching *The Ox-Bow Incident* exposes, in particular, how the fascistic strain in the Western is linked to a fear of the female: through an army ex-officer's hostility towards his effeminate son and Jane Darwell's shotgun-brandishing virago, Wellman criticizes the manic dread of appearing female that often underlies displays of toughness in the Western. In *The Ox-Bow Incident,* Wellman also denounces the castrating power of patriarchal authority, Henry Fonda's drifter finally taking part in the lynching after a piercing stare from the husband of a woman he loves issued like a challenge to his manhood. Even more extensively than Wellman, Arthur Penn has examined the Oedipal tensions of the Western. *The Left-Handed Gun,* Penn's version of the Billy the Kid legend, is a brilliant study of parricidal guilt, its hero insanely pursuing the men who killed the father figure he over-idealized. In *Little Big Man* women are a constant threat to the hero, Jack Crabb. Crabb is bullied by his wife; his foster mother, the wife of a preacher, terrifies him by her amorous advances; and his own sister wants him for her husband. It is a need to purge anxieties about his sister that prompts Crabb to seek out the fellowship of Wild Bill Hickock and spend time as a gunfighter. Only in Indian society is Crabb able to feel at home. Here he is able to marry the daughter of his Indian foster father, a woman he initially believes to be his Indian father's wife.

Rarely did the earlier Westerns openly subscribe to the wild primitive energy that Jack London had intuitively acknowledged as the authentic American sensibility. Two of the rare instances where this happened were King Vidor's *Northwest Passage* and Raoul Walsh's *They Died With Their Boots On.* Both movies celebrate an energy that can only find an outlet in madness. Unable to fit into Anglo-Saxon society, Vidor's hero finds himself condemned to embark on one mad trek into the backwoods after another, while Walsh recreates the Custer myth in accordance with the exigencies of the Errol Flynn *persona,* celebrating death in battle as the attainment of a mystical glory; 'Charge to the sound of the guns' is Custer's dictum, and this he does, renouncing all that society can offer him, until he is hacked down at the Battle of the Little Big Horn.

Raoul Walsh is the key figure in exposing the 'expressionist' intensity peculiar to American cinema. It is possible to see Walsh's work in the 'thirties and 'forties, particularly his gangster and city movies *(The Roaring Twenties, The Strawberry Blonde, High Sierra)*, as a refutation of the populist sentimentality that existed in the American cinema around the time of their appearance. An important theme of the populist cinema, to which Frank Capra *(Mr Deeds Goes to Town, Mr Smith Goes to Washington)* subscribed even more fully than the John Ford of the period, was a faith in rural America. Sentimentally presumed to possess a natural honesty and an intuitive understanding of the meaning of democracy, rural America was regarded as the keeper of the true spirit of the nation and was thought to have the potential to redeem its urban counterpart from its ruthless deviousness and slavishness to empty formalities; for credibility this optimism drew on a mythic view of Lincoln as a backwoods sage who became a guiding light for America. For Walsh, on the other hand, there is no possibility for a balanced society to exist. The heroes of his 'thirties and 'forties work, like many of his subsequent heroes, recall Capra's populist heroes in their readiness to sock on the jaw any rogues and swanks they meet, but, unlike Capra's heroes, they hardly ever dissolve the hypocrisy of the world about them through such actions; usually all that they have is the satisfaction of hitting out. Such heroes are also notably severed from rural America. They feel a kinship with nature but can never feel fully at one with it: rural and natural settings usually exist in Walsh's work to provide a temporary refuge from a threatening world. In Walsh, too, love relationships prove fragile, threatened not only by society but by the anxieties that haunt the hero. Often the *mise en scène* of a Walsh movie will make the hero seem like a lost child and the woman who loves him seem like a mother figure, as in *The Roaring Twenties* when the dead hero is mourned over on a church steps by his prostitute-mistress. Walsh's heroes, capable of only a tenuous relationship to any form of society, are driven by a need to discharge tremendous energy along a trajectory that often leads to death.

The gangster movie has always been more ready than the Western to explore the anxieties that underlie a need to display toughness. The heroes of gangster movies are often called upon to play manic travesties of fathers in fatherless families; whereas the Western hero, at least in his traditional form, is a fairly serene arbiter of patriarchal authority. To make his mother proud of him, James Cagney's Cody Jarrett in Walsh's *White Heat*, takes on the whole world – police, prison, psychiatry, everything that tries to control or regulate him. The movie ends with a sequence of extraordinary violence as Jarrett makes his last stand in a gas plant that explodes about him; having succumbed to hatred against the whole world, Jarrett imagines himself at last reunited with his mother. More than any other gangster movie, *White Heat* presents the psychopath as a symbol for the majesty of the imperatives of the self.

Since Walsh, violence and aggression have more openly established themselves as part of the tradition of American cinema. Anthony Mann is very much a companion figure to Walsh. In a string of Westerns made in the 'fifties, Mann examined extensively the kind of patriarchal repression Ford could only confront covertly in a movie like *My Darling Clementine* and with which Walsh only dealt sporadically in the Western, notably in *Pursued* and *The Lawless Breed*. Mann's Westerns deal with the traditional theme of the subjugation of insurgent elements in the name of the law. Yet there is nothing serene about the colonization of the West in these movies. Mann's Westerns present a nightmare world of sibling rivalry. On their revenge quests, his heroes can become more monstrous than the things they pursue. At times it is horror at a punishment wounding that compels the hero to become a father-like avenger (*The Man from Laramie, The Far Country*). Like Hawks, Mann is obsessed by the phallicism of weaponry and wary of anything that smacks of being female: hence the androgyny of Rock Hudson in *Bend of the River* and of Anthony Perkins in *The Tin Star* must be subordinated to a harshly pragmatic masculine code. One of the weirdest things about Mann's Westerns is the aura of utter loathsomeness and obscenity that surrounds many of the heroines. Often these women are seduced by or give themselves to the twisted enemies of the hero; the heroine in *Man of the West* is even raped by the hero's demented father figure. Mann's heroes are hardly ever able to relate to women: they usually accept a woman as their property when at the resolution of the drama they assume absolute power but there is seldom much indication that they care deeply for her. Brilliant as he was with movie actors, Mann found it difficult to direct women, especially in his Westerns; generally the actresses Mann proved able to direct were those playing women who, like forlorn mothers, finally had to lose their men to the lure of death and violence (June Allyson in *The Glen Miller Story*, Sophia Loren in *El Cid*). Since in Mann's Westerns the most forceful relationships occur between men, wounding and the infliction of pain take on an erotic force: just as Walsh's Cody Jarrett engineers his own destruction through his friendship for a police spy, Arthur Kennedy's Emerson Cole in *Bend of the River* courts death by violating his code of masculine pragmatism when he abandons James Stewart's avenger amid a wasteland instead of killing him. Although he never manages to confront fully the contradictions inherent in his vision, Mann reveals a disillusionment with the workings of power in his later non-Westerns: amidst its Walshian celebration of the delirium of combat, *El Cid* sees death as the inevitable outcome of its hero's inability to accept a wounding as proof of a basic human vulnerability; while *The Fall of the Roman Empire*, a study in parricidal intrigue, ends as hero and heroine abandon in disgust their crumbling society.

Robert Aldrich, Gordon Douglas, Sam Fuller, Phil Karlson, Don Siegel, Nicholas Ray and Martin Scorcese are other important directors who have worked in the same strain as Walsh and Mann. The main characteristics of this cinema are a fascination with extreme states of mind and the portrayal of a world so violent that love relationships find it difficult to survive. So many of the *motifs* discussed earlier recur in the work of these directors – a journey or pursuit being bound up with the evasion of woman, the psychopath who unconsciously craves death, irrational hostility towards women, the male relationship that resolves itself in violence. The heroes of these movies are often driven on by a blind need to assert themselves and whoever or whatever they pursue can appear as their own nightmare image. Thus, as in Don Siegel's *Madigan* and Sam Fuller's *Shock Corridor*, reaching the quarry, or colliding with it, can mean death or madness.

Wyatt Earp, the man with a social mission, and Doc Holliday, the fugitive from civilization – in retrospect, *My Darling Clementine* seems to have presented the traditional Western hero and his modern successor together in one movie. In Peckinpah's work, the Wyatt Earp archetype plunges deeper into disgrace and the Doc Holliday archetype achieves his supreme vindication.

'How can the prisoner reach outside except by thrusting through the wall?'

Ahab in Herman Melville's *Moby Dick*

'What is the motivation of a man who becomes a professional soldier or an outlaw? I believe it is almost always a love of violence, a deep love that proves more powerful than the lure of money, of women and of all other passion.'

Sam Peckinpah

Even if his work laments the closing of the frontier, Sam Peckinpah remains haunted by the frontier as a dynamic concept. The frontier means the vitality of Eros, atavistic frenzy, all that is lawless and free.

Most of Peckinpah's fugitive heroes head for Mexico, leaving behind them an America where life is constrained on all sides. Peckinpah loves Mexico because it is so intransigently uncivilized; at times he even shows affection for its very filthiness and dirtiness. He also has a great deal of admiration for what he considers to be the authentic Mexican mentality. Despite their tyrants and dictators, the Mexican people are seen as fundamentally free and easy, enjoying through fiestas and carousels a sensual relationship to the world about them. The Mexicans also possess the virtue of not taking money too seriously; whereas American characters often risk their lives for money, the Mexicans usually prove more inclined to face danger to defend personal honour.

The Chinese restaurant in *Ride the High Country,* the barber's shop in a saloon in *Pat Garrett and Billy the Kid* – these are settings that could only have been used by a man who knows and has studied the West. But if Peckinpah shows a great deal of affection for the West in his depiction of its past epochs, this only serves to add force to his elegy for a way of life ground down.

Peckinpah sees American history in terms of the emergence of a civilization whose main feature is wanton destructiveness, a civilization that makes man a stranger both to himself and to the world through which he moves.

For Peckinpah, puritanism has been a key force in the erosion of the frontier, having laid the foundation for future repressions by inspiring guilt and by insisting that what is wild and free must be controlled. Peckinpah often depicts puritanism as an ally of social repressions. Major Dundee in pursuit of Apache and Pat Garrett out to eliminate outlaws in the name of big business – each of these finds a zealous helper in a Bible-quoting patriarch.

Another force for the erosion of the frontier is civilized man's selfish need to exploit everything for his own ends, something which is also seen to be affecting Mexico. Some of Peckinpah's characters serve as spokesmen for the natural environment: 'These mountains don't need your trash,' Steve Judd in *Ride the High Country* warns Heck Longtree when the latter drops a paper bag on the bank of a stream; and Angel in *The Wild Bunch* rebukes Tector Gorch for calling Mexico 'just another part of Texas' by accusing him of not having eyes.

Peckinpah professes great admiration for John Huston's *The Treasure of the Sierra Madre*, and Fred C. Dobbs, its greedy hero, who makes for the Mexican hills in a demented search for gold, is for Peckinpah clearly representative of the avarice of American society in general. In Peckinpah's Mexico there are plenty of gringos out for their own ends: Gig Young's coldly efficient gangster in *Bring Me the Head of Alfredo Garcia* even jokingly gives his name as Fred C. Dobbs. At the same time, the frontier is being laid waste in the United States: the bulldozers in *Junior Bonner* appear natural heirs to Dobbs' exploitativeness.

Peckinpah depicts America's power structure as corrupt. *Major Dundee* is among other things a study of the America of the Civil War: it sees as underlying the Union's desire to defeat the South a central government's need to define a national identity through the suppression of contending power units – a view that Edmund Wilson in *Patriotic Gore* expands to explain America's involvement in external war situations like Laos. Major Dundee himself, rampaging through Mexico to satisfy private drives, is Peckinpah's commentary on Yankee arrogance. Early in the movie, we glimpse a portrait of Lincoln above Dundee's shiny black boots as they rest on a desk and it is as if Lincoln himself, America's guiding light, must bear some responsibility for Dundee's impulse to coerce all around him. In *Pat Garrett and Billy the Kid*, Peckinpah takes care to remind us that a town called Lincoln is playing a key role in the defilement of the frontier, thus exorcizing further the misguided sentimentality in American writing and films that has surrounded the figure of Lincoln.

The social orders depicted by Peckinpah are usually managed by thugs. In the Mexico of *The Treasure of the Sierra Madre* there are *federales* on the one hand and bandits on the other, but in *The Wild Bunch*, which draws heavily on Huston's picture, *federales* behave like bandits. Similarly, the Hammond brothers in *Ride the High Country* recall the villainous Clegg and Clanton clans of Ford's *Wagonmaster* and *My Darling Clementine* respectively, but, unlike them, they are not social outcasts but actually run the community where they live; in *Ride the High Country, Major Dundee* and *Pat Garrett and Billy the Kid*, R. G. Armstrong creates roles that recall his demented patriarch in Hathaway's *From Hell to Texas*, yet in Peckinpah's works, of course, he is no longer a straightforward villain of the piece but a bastion of the community.

There are plenty of tyrants and dictators in Peckinpah's cinema. Harrigan in *The Wild Bunch*, Benyon in *The Getaway* and the anonymous Chisum in *Pat Garrett and Billy the Kid* are the most nightmarish of these since the limits of their power are impossible to define; they seem to control the whole world. Society's figureheads not only menace Peckinpah's adult characters but mystify the children in his movies. The small boy who idolizes the hero has been a convention of the Western since the 'forties. However, in some cases the idolizing has led to disillusionment: in Hugo Fregonese's *The Raid*, set in a Northern town during the Civil War, a small boy hero-worships a man who eventually turns out to be a Southern spy bent on destroying the community. In Peckinpah's work, hero-worship is seen as totally misguided. In *The Wild Bunch* it is Mapache, the cruel Mexican dictator, who is worshipped by a small boy and in the final showdown the same child actually guns down Pike Bishop, the noble outlaw leader, whom he automatically classes as an enemy.

An important contribution by William Wellman to the Western was the technique of creating unsettling effects by dissolving moods of social stability. This technique was subsequently continued by such directors as Anthony Mann and Don Siegel. Peckinpah again takes it up in his movies. At times he refers us directly back to Wellman: recalling Wellman's *Across the Wide Missouri*, Christmas festivities in *Major Dundee* are marred by the eruption of violence, and *The Wild Bunch*, like Wellman's *Yellow Sky*, opens with a group of soldiers riding into a town and then turning out to be outlaws in disguise.

A feeling that the world is a contradictory place informs the whole of Peckinpah's work. On the one hand, documentary realism recreates past epochs: Pancho Villa's attack on Mapache in *The Wild Bunch* was shot after photographs of an actual battle during the Mexican Revolution. On the other hand, some of Peckinpah's scenes are totally surreal: no one could claim as naturalistic the reverend's damnation sermon during a church social in *Straw Dogs*. On other occasions, the antithetical nature of the world can be evident within a single shot: in *The Getaway*, the final regeneration of the love between Doc McCoy and his wife has a garbage dump for a backdrop. Peckinpah also takes us back to Melville and Hawthorne in the manner he often expands allegorical elements to accommodate a multi-layered symbolism: the representational functions of both the Apache and American flag in *Major Dundee* change depending on which narrative strand we view each of these from, while Cable in *The Ballad of Cable Hogue* refers both to Cain and Abel as evidence of the confused state of human nature.

A desire to present life as a disorientating experience for his characters accounts for much of Peckinpah's *mise en scène*. Unlike DeMille and Ford, Peckinpah never groups his characters together to create the impression of a world that is a cohesive whole. Usually Peckinpah presents his characters strung across the frame, and if he groups characters together, it is usually to present the community or some social group as a hostile force bearing down upon his central characters – a technique that recalls Nicholas Ray, notably in *Johnny Guitar* and *The True Story of Jesse James*. Peckinpah's handling of a moving camera is at its most stunning when he uses it to convey the subjective dimension of terror that can isolate his heroines from the world about them: as in Elsa Knudsen's entry into the mining-camp brothel in *Ride the High Country*, the camera moving hesitantly around groups of mocking faces; or in Carol Benyon's search for the lost bankroll at a railway station in *The Getaway*, her searching face overlain with the noise of a baby crying and intercut with pans around noisy but impassive faces.

Peckinpah's heroes are men who have no tie nor bond to the world through which they move. They are mostly social outcasts, some of them even outlaws, and they stand for an America that is denied any effective self-expression. Only in *Junior Bonner* is a Peckinpah hero seen in terms of a family and then this proves so eroded by social change that it can provide no stability. Ford's heroes usually have memories of the past to console them when life becomes difficult, but Peckinpah's do not even have this: when they muse about the past, it is to speak of friends who have ended up dying shabbily, deceived and betrayed by the world. Moreover, it is because they cling to a freedom that is gone that they are so estranged. Steve Judd in *Ride the High Country* imagining the applause of crowds for a camel race is actually for him; or Ace Bonner in *Junior Bonner* reminiscing how the whole of Madison Square Garden stood and cheered when he once rode a bull – these men still demand the acknowledgement of their natural dignity in a world that has sworn allegiance to a political and business aristocracy. Visibly ageing, they stand for a vitality that is fading before the dullness of modern society.

Leslie Fiedler has pointed out that Mark Twain's Huckleberry Finn, with his intuitive commitment to flee the constraints of civilization, was probably the first existentialist hero. Existentialist is a term that has at times been applied to Peckinpah's work, and if it can be made to fit, it is, as with Huck Finn, in terms of the natural self asserting itself. Most of Peckinpah's Westerns recall Ford's *My Darling Clementine* in that they have dual male protagonists, one of whom stands for order while the other asserts the imperatives of the self. Tyreen and Dundee in *Major Dundee*, Pike Bishop and Deke Thornton in

The Wild Bunch – these are the pairs in Peckinpah's work that perhaps most strongly resemble Ford's Doc Holliday and Wyatt Earp. But, more openly than Ford ever does, Peckinpah reveals the dualism as a conflict between nature and society. Moreover, Peckinpah's Wyatt Earp figures prove unable to renounce the primitive power of the frontier and through his Doc Holliday figures the movies move forward to expressions of disaffiliation from community values.

Social integration for the Peckinpah's heroes is tantamount to a kind of imprisonment; many even spend time in prison. The manacled and outraged Tyreen in his prison cell in *Major Dundee*; the flogged and sweaty body of Deke Thornton in the penal colony in *The Wild Bunch*; Ollinger, Pat Garrett's zealously religious deputy, ramming a shotgun in the chest of a handcuffed Billy the Kid, who refuses to believe in God; Doc McCoy in *The Getaway*, condemned to the mechanical ritual of the penitentiary – such scenes powerfully evoke moods of repression and frustration.

A rejection of Anglo-Saxon notions of propriety runs through Peckinpah's work. In Ford's movies, horseplay never exceeds the bounds of moderation: indeed, a fist-fight can appear a community ritual, with the ladies looking on and a patriarch acting as referee. Closer to 'the true men' of whom Stephen Crane wrote, Peckinpah's male characters can cut loose completely: in *The Wild Bunch* the Gorch brothers' orgy with whores amid wine-vats is only brought to an end through exhaustion. Peckinpah clearly admires the way his more roguish characters, like the Gorch brothers, gleefully flaunt a lack of propriety that the conventionally-minded find disgusting. In *Pat Garrett and Billy the Kid* moral distinctions are actually reinforced in terms of hygiene; the free and easy outlaws are scruffy, bedraggled and slouch about, while the minions of a corrupt government, like Pat Garrett and his deputies, appear repellent with all their clean attire and the poise with which they bear themselves.

Peckinpah has no regard for the Western's traditional view of women. Sometimes he conjures up the spectre of a demure heroine for the pleasure of exorcising it. Claudia, the Deaddog housewife in *The Ballad of Cable Hogue*; the reverend's superficially charming wife in *Straw Dogs* – these are exposed as morally hypocritical and certainly provide no reason to distrust sexual frankness in other women. Peckinpah's heroines often appear closer to nature than his male characters. He hardly ever defines them in terms of home or community; like the Indian girl in the Western, their true habitat appears to be the world of nature, and they are often depicted with paradisal images, being linked in particular with streams and rivers. What his heroines have in common, most of them prostitutes and Mexican beauties, is an inability to renounce the flesh. In the more ordinary Hollywood movies, actresses merely insinuate their sexuality, but Peckinpah ensures that his actresses are given the opportunity of ramming theirs at the audience: as with the awesome sight of Senta Berger's dripping body emerging from the pool in *Major Dundee;* the close-up flashbacks to Stella Stevens' bosom in *The Ballad of Cable Hogue;* or the recurrent spectacle of Isela Vega's nakedness in *Bring Me the Head of Alfredo Garcia.* Indeed, Peckinpah seems unable simply to *suggest* female sensuality: Susan George displaying her naked torso at a window in *Straw Dogs* is somewhat out of character and appears a rather crude way on Peckinpah's part of showing that she is a coquette.

An important aspect of Peckinpah's work, but one overlooked, is its Gothic element. This element lends his work a particular richness. None of his movies are Gothic in a hermetically sealed manner, like the stories of Edgar Allan Poe; rather the Gothic is always seen in relation to other concerns, notably in a celebration of the sheer physicality of life. Whereas John Ford could handle Gothic themes without really exploring them, Peckinpah's preoccupations squarely spring from a desire to investigate the mechanics of repression.

Melville's Ahab and Twain's Huckleberry Finn both felt themselves to be damned through listening to the promptings of their own inner natures, while in Stephen Crane's verse to love is to be chastised by the wrath of God. Peckinpah's work is suffused with a similar mood of unjust damnation. Cable Hogue and Junior Bonner are the Peckinpah heroes whose behaviour is least impaired by the civilizing process going on around them; in them the vital promptings of the frontier are still able to express themselves with a relative freedom. Steve Judd, Major Dundee, Pike Bishop, or Bennie in *Alfredo Garcia* – these men stand at the other end of the scale, their personalities have absorbed too many of society's inflexible values not to be to some degree distorted; they are cut off from their fellows by the need to live off inner dramas of suffering. Deep within themselves, they feel that they are eternally damned; wherever they journey, all they can really see are vistas compounded out of their own pain.

So much of the behaviour of Peckinpah's heroes – the fits of melancholy, the fear about trusting, the sheltering behind authoritarian attitudes – can be put down to an exclusion from love. We can never imagine any of his heroes having experienced a childhood; rather they all seem to have been ripped from the womb and thrust into a world of struggle. A conventional way to open a Western is to present in long shot its hero riding across a plain and then to move in closer on him. Peckinpah, however, introduces the heroes of his Westerns by thrusting them upon the audience: such men appear as if out of nowhere in the midst of some disconcerting situation. They are always on the go. Sometimes they are even denied the opportunity to sleep: *The Glory Guys*, which Peckinpah scripted, opens with a soldier waking up from a nightmare; in the opening of *The Wild Bunch*, Deke Thornton is woken up by the news that his men are about to ambush Pike Bishop; and in the scene that follows the opening credits of *Pat Garrett and Billy the Kid*, the morning awakening of Billy the Kid and a couple of friends is occasioned by the gunfire of Garrett's posse.

In depicting a world that is strongly patriarchal, Peckinpah not so much details the frustration of the maternal principle as mourns this frustration. Mothers are never able to fulfil their roles properly: in *Alfredo Garcia* a mother can only look on mutely as her daughter is tortured, while in *Pat Garrett and Billy the Kid* Mrs Horrell is prevented from giving Billy a meal by the eruption of violence. Even more extensively than Walsh, Peckinpah seeks to present his heroes as sons excluded from maternal warmth. A child's unease often provides us with a perspective from which to see these heroes: *Major Dundee* opens with a small boy calling for his mother as he is abducted by Indians, and in *The Wild Bunch* there is a zoom-out to Mexican military manoeuvres from a baby suckled at a mother's breast crossed by cartridge belts.

Peckinpah recalls directors like Mann, Penn, Walsh, Wellman and Thorpe in that for certain of his heroes women provide occasions for encounters with patriarchal authority, toughness being something displayed to mask Oedipal anxieties. To men like the Wild Bunch, Major Dundee, Doc McCoy in *The Getaway*, Bennie in *Alfredo Garcia*, women are linked with the mother; some of their women are prostitutes and those that are not give or have given themselves to another man, often a figure of authority. Hence, one reason why many of these heroes behave in a tough or authoritarian manner with their women is because they resent them; they see their women as potential betrayers, forever capable of going over to the side of a menacing authority.

Peckinpah's cinema is filled with scenes of rape and attempted rape. On a subliminal level, such scenes appear nightmare renderings of the primal scene. As such they underline the exclusion of Peckinpah's heroes from maternal warmth: in *Pat Garrett and Billy the Kid* the sight of a Mexican girl being raped is even accompanied by that of her baby crying. These scenes of nightmare coitus also clarify the manner in which these men fear their own sexual potential: in *Straw Dogs* the rape of Sumner's wife helps us to understand the incest terrors that hinder Sumner's own relationship with her; while to Major Dundee the rape of the Rostes' women is linked to the transgressor he unconsciously fears in himself. Like Henry Fonda's drifter in Wellman's *The Ox-Bow Incident*, they are haunted by the piercing stare of patriarchal authority. Only in *Ride the High Country* does an actual father interrupt love-making, Joshua Knudsen intruding upon the nocturnal meeting of his daughter and Heck Longtree; yet numerous other scenes – the woundings of Major Dundee and Pike Bishop, for instance – subliminally suggest how attempts at love-making are frustrated by the castrating power of patriarchal authority. In *The Searchers*, Ford deals with the incest taboo within a rigid family structure, subscribing unreflectively to the view that the difference between the relaxation and enforcement of such a taboo is the difference between anarchy and order. Peckinpah, however, understands the destructive potential of the incest taboo and he dismisses the kind of repressive conscience that a patriarchal society can instil in the mind of the individual. For him, the essential conflict lies not between anarchy and order but between a person's natural right to copulate and the capacity of a patriarchal society to poison the libido even before it has had a chance to live. Peckinpah's cinema is a total denunciation of a world where the father is such an awesome figure that the threat of castration proves a devastating experience for the male psyche.

If Peckinpah has great admiration for the foul-mouthed behaviour of men like the Gorch brothers and can himself reject Anglo-Saxon notions of propriety, there also runs through his work as a counter-theme the realization that a man does not beat any form of society by simply telling it to go to hell; rather to achieve freedom, he must penetrate to the depths of his own psyche and from there exorcize the demons of repression. It is thus appropriate that there is a touch of irony to Peckinpah's celebration of nature and the basic things of life. If the pastorial and paradisial in his work act as a reminder of the fulsome physicality of life, they also prove places of insubstantial refuge from an unmanageable world; and if Peckinpah's women can be richly corporeal, they can also be shadowy creatures – indeed, many of his secondary women characters are rather like figments of male masturbatory fantasies, being around only so that the male characters can copulate with them. Yet such men's room elements are ultimately located in a reflective framework through Peckinpah's analysis of patriarchal oppression.

Peckinpah's occasional treatment of Mexico as a dream reality recalls Arthur Penn's depiction of Indian society in *Little Big Man.* Taking the Western convention of a hero who loves an Indian girl with the approval of Indian society, Penn shows that this stands for a fantasy enactment of incest. Similarly, Peckinpah presents his dream world Mexico in relation to a patriarchal America; both Pike Bishop in *The Wild Bunch* and Billy the Kid have gentle Mexican 'fathers' and find Mexican women sexually pliant – these men, so it seems, could enter Eden but for the anxieties that they carry within them.

In his non-Westerns *(Bonnie and Clyde, Alice's Restaurant)*, Penn is able to proceed from a contemplation of masculine frustrations to an elegy for a womankind that must remain sexually unfulfilled. Peckinpah, on the other hand, remains predominantly interested in masculine frustrations throughout his work, yet there are moments when he briefly pays tribute to a forlorn womanhood, as with Amy's renunciation of Locken in *The Killer Elite*, Billy the Kid's Mexican girlfriend in mourning over Billy's corpse, Hildy confronted with the dying Cable Hogue, or Eva forsaken by Steiner in *Cross of Iron.*

Sexual impotence has often been strangely linked with an approval of toughness by American artists, as with Hemingway in *The Sun Also Rises* or Hawks in *Tiger Shark.* As a reaction against the debilitating pressures of Anglo-

Saxon society, Vidor in *Northwest Passage* and Mailer-Walsh in *The Naked and the Dead* actually approve a violent energy in their heroes; as might be expected from a man who understands so well the workings of sexual repression in the Western, Peckinpah shares with Walsh and Vidor a love of the primitive energy of the frontier, and like them, Peckinpah takes us back to Jack London in the Nietzschean quality of this love, and his work is perhaps the cinema's most eloquent defence of the fury to which so many American artists have felt intuitively committed as the authentic American sensibility.

A number of critics have objected to Peckinpah's love of violence. But for a man who wants to make Westerns and yet fervently believes that human dignity has nothing whatsoever to do with social trappings, what else is there to do but love violence? So many of Peckinpah's heroes feel the most accursed among all creation for most of their lives, but when they submit to violence and the fury of the frontier floods their psyches, these men can feel only dignity.

Violence in Peckinpah is proof that men will live at extremes, go mad, do anything, just to feel truly alive. That *Alfredo Garcia* should begin with a pastoral idyll and end with death and bloodshed is no accident; the two are connected in that the paroxysm of violence is a product of the denial of the idyll. By preferring the attraction of violence to that of financial gain and all the false security this can bring, Peckinpah's heroes affirm that they are immune from the blandishments of American capitalism. By choosing violence, they prove that the libido is not yet dead within them despite the fact that social repression has excluded them from women.

Violence is always memorably shot in Peckinpah's movies. Recalling Walsh in *White Heat* or Nicholas Ray in *The True Story of Jesse James*, Peckinpah often begins a movie with a sequence of rapid cutting that leads into an explosion of violence. Like Mann, Peckinpah can give added impact to a scene of wounding by encapsulating a gun being fired and a person being shot within a single frame – perhaps the most extraordinary instance of this occurs in *The Wild Bunch* when Pike Bishop is shot in the back by a woman. A feeling of nirvana attained, of 'super-reality' exploding forth, suffuses Peckinpah's scenes of violence, and since *The Wild Bunch* this effect has owed a great deal to the director's use of slow motion. Slow motion exaggerates the non-naturalistic manner of the cutting for scenes of violence, especially when Peckinpah cuts away from a body falling in slow motion, only to return to it later as it hits the ground. Rather than disrupting the narrative flow, this cutting enables it to achieve a dream-like intensity.

Peckinpah's heroes are motivated by a similar need to discharge aggression to those of more traditional Western directors, only they claim no social pretexts for their actions. Ford's Ethan Edwards in *The Searchers* could always excuse his mad pursuit of the Apache by claiming his actions were socially useful, yet for Peckinpah's Major Dundee the pursuit of the Apache finally becomes an end itself. Similarly, whereas in Hawks' *Rio Bravo* John Wayne and his buddies affirm their solidarity by jubilantly discharging aggression in the name of the law against the villains of the piece, Billy the Kid and his friends in Peckinpah's *Pat Garrett and Billy the Kid* merely affirm their togetherness by shooting at chicken in a chicken-shoot. In fact, the male group in Peckinpah's work is more defiantly a custodian of Eros than in the work of any other American director.

For his handling of violence, Peckinpah has often been compared to Arthur Penn. Yet for Penn's heroes violence is never noble, only furtive. Bubber Reeves in *The Chase*, Clyde in *Bonnie and Clyde*, Billy the Kid in *The Left-Handed Gun* – for them a violent death provides a convenient escape from the dilemma of a repressed homosexuality. For the latter two, a violent death is also clearly the penalty for craving union with the mother – Clyde rushing to Bonnie so he can die by her side, Billy the Kid dying after being rejected by a married woman he seduced. A dread of patriarchal authority ensures that Penn's heroes must remain arrested adolescents and can never attain sexual maturity. On such grounds, *Little Big Man*, for all its insight, is finally morally evasive, since when Jack Crabb comes upon Custer, he is unable to plunge his knife into him because this gesture – Custer is naked and grooming himself – would force him to confront his own sexual proclivities. A number of Peckinpah's heroes recall Penn's in that they are repressed homosexuals – Pike Bishop in *The Wild Bunch*, Billy the Kid, Bennie in *Alfredo Garcia* are the most obvious of these. Yet death for them is not the cowardly escape that it is for Penn's heroes; exceeding Mann even more than Penn in the erotic force he gives to wounding, Peckinpah ensures that death comes as a testament to the power of Eros – his heroes are at last no longer afraid of who they are. Moreover, if death for such men can be the occasion for an attempted reunion with the mother (both Bishop and Billy the Kid must die after bouts of love-making), it is also an outcry against the patriarchal tyranny that has made the mother a distant figure. Even Billy the Kid, the most passive of Peckinpah's heroes, has some understanding that the law is cruel which demands his death – an awareness Penn's Billy the Kid never achieves. Some of Peckinpah's heroes even commit acts tantamount to parricide before they die. Pike Bishop gunning down Mapache, the Mexican dictator; Bennie killing El Jefe, a Mexican patriarch – each of these has a moment during his final spiral into madness, when he is able to pull back and reflect on his state of mind, only to conclude that he would not have it any other way. Of all the directors who since Walsh have responded to the mystique of the psychopath mentality, Peckinpah is the one most wholeheartedly to endorse the imperatives of the self and as such his work constitutes an exorcizing of the filial piety that the Western in particular and American cinema in general have traditionally seen as the fitting reaction to patriarchal oppression.

Peckinpah has claimed the writings of Jean-Paul Sartre have influenced his work. Yet the existentialist strain in Peckinpah's work remains firmly based in innate natural drives and he has little of Sartre's concern with a reflective consciousness. Hence *Straw Dogs*, which draws heavily on *The Flies* and is Peckinpah's most self-consciously Sartrian movie, is the director's biggest failure; Peckinpah's fascination with a mind in a state of flux prevents him from fulfilling his aim of producing a hero who can introduce value into the world in a rational manner. Nevertheless, it is easy to see why Peckinpah should be enthusiastic about *The Flies* since the play is a vindication of violence against the family, being the story of a young man who returns to his home-town to liberate it from tyranny by killing his mother and step-father. The play's influence is less obtrusively perceptible in a number of Peckinpah's other movies: the violent finale of *Alfredo Garcia*, for instance, is presented as a symbolic home-coming for the hero. In *The Wild Bunch*, Sartrian influence is perhaps best assimilated: in basing his heroes' last stand on the mad last stand of Sartre's hero in *Iron in the Soul*, Peckinpah is drawing upon a strain of romantic rebellion in Sartre with which he himself is in tune.

Out to square off against the parental authority of the culture that produced them, Peckinpah's isolated heroes are among the American cinema's most direct descendants of Melville's Ahab. Ahab has his harpoon to revenge himself on Moby Dick, to whom he has lost a leg. Similarly, Peckinpah's heroes often have wounds – Pike Bishop and Major Dundee leg wounds, Yellowleg a wounded arm, Mike Locken both a wounded arm and leg – and they take a vengeful delight in the phallicism of weaponry: they brandish their guns at the least opportunity, not just to conceal sexual fears, but as a gesture of defiance against the authority that has engendered these fears.

As with Melville's Ahab, the tragedy of so many of Peckinpah's heroes is their isolation from their fellow men; often it is only before death that they realize the value of human companionship. In this respect, Peckinpah's work is a criticism of the Western's Emersonian individualism and its attendant protestantism. Like Melville also, Peckinpah believes in the need for catharsis: in his chaotic world, conventional morality can never exert a positive control, and the rediscovery of harmony is only possible through tensions being lived out. Hence his commitment to the maternal principle, the heart, as opposed to the paternal principle, the head; what his heroes intuitively crave in their wrath is for the mother to assume the role of a force for leniency and loosening-up in the culture about them.

Peckinpah continually rejects DeMille's tacit championship of repressive controls: for him all forms of repression are essentially irrelevant since it is actually from repression that disorder spings. We may be shocked by the violent destructions of the frontier township in *The Wild Bunch* and the Cornish community in *Straw Dogs*, yet we acknowledge such outbursts are a necessary means of reactivating dead matter. For Peckinpah the content of a particular social structure always has the right to determine the outer form of that structure.

Whereas Cable Hogue will on no account renounce the freedom of the frontier, Doc McCoy in *The Getaway*, Mike Locken in *The Killer Elite* and Steiner in *Cross of Iron* rediscover a similar freedom by living out the contradictions of the violence within them. To cross from repression over into freedom, this is what drives so many of Peckinpah's heroes on. And if a number of them can only hit the divide between the twain to be blasted into complete madness, nothing in the world can prevent them from trying to make the transition. Trapped in a world that is a deformity, men like Steve Judd and Pike Bishop finally choose to perish as martyrs in the cause of a love that can know no barriers. They may appear anachronisms, but they stand for the hope of the future in that they seek to liberate themselves at all cost from the repressions of the past.

CHAPTER ONE: THE DEADLY COMPANIONS

or Sam Peckinpah versus Maureen O'Hara

The Deadly Companions was produced by Maureen O'Hara's brother, who appears to have seen the picture primarily as a vehicle for his sister. Peckinpah took the job as director because he wanted to work with Brian Keith, with whom he had already worked on a television series called *The Westerner*. Peckinpah claims that he found the movie a trying experience since his directorial freedom was severely constrained: he was apparently allowed to do little more than tinker with the script and he was given little opportunity to direct Maureen O'Hara's performance. Thus, the first part of the movie is the strongest, dealing as it does largely with the characters played by Keith, Chill Wills and Steve Cochran.

The Deadly Companions has one of Peckinpah's most memorable openings. First we see the feet of Yellowleg (Brian Keith) as he enters a saloon, a yellow stripe down his trouser leg establishing him as an ex-Union soldier. Then the camera pans past a group of men playing cards to the feet of a man strung up from the ceiling. The man is revealed as Turk (Chill Wills), who is being punished for cheating at cards. This opening brilliantly underlines the disconcerting effect the encounter with Turk has on Yellowleg. Yellowleg was scalped by Turk during the Civil War and has spent years tracking him down to take his scalp in revenge; but now, at last confronted with Turk, Yellowleg suddenly realizes that if he fulfils his obsession he will destroy the only purpose that his life has.

Despite the card-players' cries of 'Stay out of this, Yank', Yellowleg cuts Turk down. Until such a time as he feels able to take his revenge, Yellowleg decides to annex himself to Turk; and claiming he knows a nearby bank that will be easy to rob, he rides off with Turk and Turk's young sidekick, Billy (Steve Cochran).

Turk and Billy are among Peckinpah's most bizarre rogues. Turk is the first in a line of 'castrating father figures' in Peckinpah's work, although unlike his successors (Mapache in *The Wild Bunch* or Benyon in *The Getaway)*, he has no social institutions to back him up. Turk loves power more than anything else in the world. He covets a general's cap, a trophy from the war, and often shows this to Billy, telling him of his dream to found a kingdom called 'Fredonia' where there would be 'a lot of laws but none of them would apply to us'. In this kingdom Turk would be able to set himself up at the head of a massive army and lead it on rampages wherever he wanted. The character of Billy serves as a complement to that of Yellowleg. Whereas Yellowleg feels he can never again know a woman's love because of Turk's scalping of him, Billy seeks to dominate women as a means of concealing anxieties that spring from his own relationship to Turk: when we first see him, Billy has surrounded himself by prostitutes, and later he feels compelled to assert his manhood by trying to rape Kit (Maureen O'Hara). As the film progresses, Billy is drawn to Yellowleg as if to an older brother. Finally revealing that he too nurtures a mad hatred for the old man, Billy urges Yellowleg to kill Turk in the movie's climax.

Turk and Billy, however, are less unpleasant than the citizens of the townships through which they and Yellowleg ride; indeed, even Yellowleg's vengeance gains some justification in that in some ways it appears to spring from a refusal to adapt to the kind of society that has come into being after the Civil War. Turk and Billy are at least not coldly rational in their cruelty; unlike the men in the saloon at the beginning of the movie, they would not string a man up and then calmly sit around and play cards as he suffers. Similarly, Billy might try to rape Kit, but he is incapable of the cynical indifference that the citizens of Gila City show to her when they let her go alone into Indian country to bury her dead son by her husband's grave.

In what is possibly the finest scene in the picture, Billy and Turk totally expose the hypocrisy of the people of Gila City. Along with Yellowleg, they stroll into Gila City's saloon one Sunday morning. The bar is closing because a religious service is to be held in the saloon, and the bartender pulls a drape down over the painting of a nude Billy and Turk have begun to admire: 'Parson don't like to look at it during his sermon,' he explains. When the service begins, it is interrupted by Turk demanding to no avail that he still has the right to a drink. Then Turk begins to ramble on to Billy about his dream army, '*Johnny Comes Marching Home*' striking up on the sound-track as a counterpoint to the '*Rock of Ages*' of the service. Called upon by the parson to remove his hat Yellowleg leaves rather than do so and reveal the wounds from Turk's scalping. Billy, however, refuses to be intimidated in any way: 'If they're going to heaven, let you and me not go,' he moans to Turk about the congregation; and when the parson makes a request that anyone who wishes to go to hell should stand up, Billy does so, even firing his gun in defiance. Then he walks up to Kit Tilden, the local prostitute, and gives her a kiss. The whole congregation is thrown into confusion by Billy's conduct.

The kind of *persona* that Maureen O'Hara has established on the screen has been characterized by its 'homeliness'; thus, while O'Hara is excellent as the archetypal Ford wife-mother in *Wings of Eagles* and *Rio Grande*, she is not the kind of actress one can imagine playing a prostitute. Predictably perhaps, she plays the part of Kit Tilden as if Kit were one of Ford's noble prostitute figures – the Dallas of *Stagecoach* or the Dorothy Jordan of *The Sun Shines Bright*. To O'Hara Kit is clearly a woman who is basically ashamed of what she is and yearns to be like so-called decent folk – exactly the kind of woman, that is, who would be a hypocrite in the Sam Peckinpah canon. When O'Hara has Kit outraged by Billy's kiss during the sermon in the saloon, she obviously thinks that she is having Kit make the only gesture possible to assert some claim to dignity; yet her Kit actually appears to be displaying something similar to the high-minded disdain of the townspeople who resent her. Similarly, O'Hara appears to see in Kit's trek to bury her dead son beside her husband an earnest attempt by Kit to lay claim to dignity in the community's eyes; seen in the context of Peckinpah's satire on Gila City's notions of propriety, however, Kit's action only emerges as neurotic and unbalanced.

In the cinema of Sam Peckinpah, humanization and socialization appear as two distinctly different things. Humanization is where an individual gains moral awareness through contact with other individuals, while socialization is where an individual is called upon to aquiesce to pre-existing codes of conduct. In *The Deadly Companions* Kit's son is a force for Yellowleg's humanization. Yellowleg's killing of the boy, with whom he has struck up a friendship, is a consequence of his obsession with revenge. Caught up in a gunfight with men who are already robbing the bank he and his companions intended to rob, Yellowleg is unable to aim his gun properly due to an unattended war wound and his bullet accidentally hits the boy. After the shoot-out, Yellowleg pensively retrieves the boy's mouth-organ from the town's dusty main-street, forced to confront the absurdity and meaninglessness of his obsession with revenge.

In contrast to her son, Kit herself, with her mindless acceptance of repressive notions of propriety, seems largely a force for Yellowleg's socialization. It is hard for us to feel that Yellowleg and Kit genuinely warm to one another, Maureen O'Hara's playing of her part being uniformly cold and formal. Whereas through bathing other Peckinpah heroines express a physical delight in themselves, a moonlight bathe by O'Hara serves to be merely decorative.

The second part of the movie is at its best when it depicts Yellowleg's fascination with violence. In what is perhaps the movie's most famous scene, Yellowleg watches a stagecoach come hurtling by him and Kit; it is manned by Indians who have dressed themselves as whites and are indulging in an orgy of drunkenness. Finally the stage overturns, leaving its occupants lying exhausted around it. Throughout this scene, we share with Yellowleg a delight in the delirium of savagery.

If Yellowleg and Kit's love story is vaguely convincing, it is thanks to the basic mechanics of the plot. Yellowleg feels compelled to accompany Kit on the trek and he stays by her even after Billy and Turk have gone back to Gila City to try again to rob the bank. Symbolically at least, Kit's killing of a pursuing Indian signifies her destruction of the mad animal in Yellowleg. When Yellowleg and Kit reach the ghost town where Kit's husband lies buried, they are surprised by Turk and Billy, who have now robbed the Gila City bank.

Yellowleg is forced to seek his revenge, Turk mockingly interrupting as he kisses Kit and thus aggravating the castration impact of the scalping. Here the movie has been marred by producer's alterations. According to the original script, Yellowleg should have gunned down Billy, thus himself taking up arms against the destructiveness of his personality. Now it is Turk himself who shoots Billy in a gesture which is totally out of character. The climax comes to an end when Yellowleg relents from scalping Turk thanks to Kit's insistence that she can love him in spite of his scars.

The ending of *The Deadly Companions* is given a fillip by the arrival at the ghost town of people from Gila City. Although none of them would accompany Kit on her trek, they have now ridden out as a posse to retrieve their stolen money; even the parson is among them. 'You know how people are, as long as it's their money, the gates of hell wouldn't stop them,' the sheriff comments. Confronted again by the hypocrisy of Gila City, we can only have doubts about socialization as a way of providing a meaning to Yellowleg's life – if, in fact, Kit has finally succeeded in socializing him. Appropriately, the movie ends on a note of stalemate as Kit and Yellowleg ride away, leaving us with no idea where they are going. Considering the circumstances under which the movie was made, Peckinpah's greatest achievement in *The Deadly Companions* is possibly his failure to integrate his themes: called upon to tell a love story that recalls the relationship of Ford's Wyatt Earp and Clementine, Peckinpah just cannot bring himself to do it.

CHAPTER TWO: RIDE THE HIGH COUNTRY

Critics have tended to view *Ride the High Country* as a Western of a more traditional kind than it actually is, presumably because it proves such a fine vehicle for the farewell performances of Joel McCrea and Randolph Scott. But the moral complexity that results from character interaction and the bitter edge to its elegy for the decline of the frontier make it more than the companion-piece to *True Grit* it has frequently been called.

The movie opens by establishing a conflict between nature and civilization. Credits roll over scenery of extraordinary beauty: mountains, rivers, pine forests – all devoid of people. Then Peckinpah switches to a town at carnival time: crowds of people in eastern garb throng around stalls that exploit the heritage of the frontier and the lure of foreign parts as gimmicks to make money.

At the carnival, Steve Judd encounters Gil Westrum and Heck Longtree, both of whom exhibit debased frontier values. Westrum is an old friend of Judd's and also an ex-lawman; but, unlike Judd, he is out to survive in the modern world; he now spends his time running a rifle-range, trophies from his frontier days drawing people to his stall. Longtree, Westrum's young side-kick, provides an example of force in the service of mercenary values as, after winning a race on a camel against horses, he flings himself into a fight with a man to collect a bet.

A familiar grouping in Westerns is the sight of a tall hero in mid-frame flanked by secondary characters, and Peckinpah exploits this to achieve pathos in a scene where Judd visits a bank that wishes to employ him, the short, pot-bellied banker and his scrawny, middle-aged son positioned on either side of the tall but slightly bowed figure of Judd. A comic but ultimately sad contrast is drawn between the hesitant behaviour of the banker and the resoluteness of Judd. The banker, taken aback that Judd is not a younger man, cannot make up his mind whether to give Judd a job transporting gold, and it is only Judd's insistence on his own capabilities that wins him the job.

The other modes of civilization presented in *Ride the High Country* are as unattractive as the township with which the movie opens. As Judd sets off for the mining camp of Coarse Gold to pick up gold, he is joined by Gil Westrum and Heck Longtree, whose help he has enlisted; and the three of them come upon the Knudsen farmstead. The Knudsen farmstead is a place where the head rules and the heart is outlawed, the Bible-quoting and tyrannical Joshua Knudsen lording it over his home. Knudsen has buried his dead and unfaithful wife right next to the farmhouse, an inscription on the grave making public her shame. In seeking to be the enemy of all feeling, Knudsen has plunged himself into terror and despair; the more he seeks to subjugate feeling in himself, the more this seeks to break out in an incestuous longing for his own daughter, Elsa. Thus, Knudsen unconsciously sees any suitor of Elsa's as a reflection of a transgressor in himself and can only feel hatred at this. During meal-time in the Knudsen household, Heck Longtree begins to feel attracted towards Elsa but dare do no more than exchange furtive glances with her, and later a nocturnal meeting he arranges with her is rudely interrupted by Knudsen, the patriarch's demented face emerging out of the darkness.

What law exists in the mining-camp of Coarse Gold is administered by the drunken Judge Tolliver, who merely legalizes the actions of whoever happens to be the strongest. It is not just the brutality of the people of Coarse Gold that is disturbing, but also their insensitivity to one another's suffering. When Tolliver is beaten up in the town brothel by the Hammond brothers, Peckinpah's camera lingers on two prostitutes: one, the judge's girl, is in tears, but the other sits devouring meat, completely indifferent to what is happening.

Joshua Knudsen warns Judd and his companions that Coarse Gold is a den of depravity; yet it is the kind of attitudes Knudsen upholds that in many ways appear responsible for the camp's condition. If the five Hammond brothers recall in their surliness the villainous clans of Ford (the Cleggs in *Wagonmaster* and the Clantons in *My Darling Clementine)*, they are distinguished from them in that their clan has no father to lead it; the Hammond brothers are essentially sons in revolt against a tyrannical father. They assert a conspiratorial solidarity by sharing one another's women, each woman they meet seemingly a mother to be degraded in defiance of patriarchal authority.

Annexing herself to Judd's troop, Elsa Knudsen flees home and comes to Coarse Gold to marry Billy Hammond. The Hammond brothers respond to her arrival at the camp with horseplay. Elsa's wedding with Billy the brothers see merely as an occasion to demonstrate fraternal loyalty; they ride into town boldly singing a song about their prowess and after the ceremony two of them attempt to rape Elsa but are restrained by the intervention of Judd and Heck. Cutting between the attempted rape of Elsa and scenes of brawling in the saloon where the wedding is held, Peckinpah for the first time in his work uses a montage technique to create the impression of energy exploding.

The function of the Hammond brothers in the movie finally proves purgative: it is they who end the tyranny of Joshua Knudsen, erupting into his home like the rebellious instincts he fears. We learn of Knudsen's death in a manner that brilliantly exposes the duplicity of the Knudsen farmstead. Framing Knudsen supposedly praying at his wife's grave, Peckinpah zooms in on Knudsen's face which we discover has a bullet between its eyes; then he cuts to the farmhouse where the Hammonds are in defiant occupation.

Peckinpah claims that the original screenplay for *Ride the High Country*, which he rewrote, was a fairly conventional piece of work. What conventional elements now remain in the movie exist to be subverted. With Westrum's revelation that he intends to relieve Judd of the gold, the movie appears to be settling into familiar territory – a hero on the side of the law and an old friend out to turn to crime. But the Manichean implications of the plotline are totally undercut: the 'good' guy is not without imperfections, while the 'bad' guy has a lot that can be said in his favour. Usually Westerns that attack the Manicheanism of the genre are distinguished by misanthropy: the final message of a *Waterhole* 3 or a *There was a Crooked Man* is that everybody is bad and corrupt, not just those society classes as such. Peckinpah's movie, however, remains resolutely humanist: Peckinpah still believes in human potential; it is just that Manichean notions provide no means of appreciating such potential.

If Steve Judd maintains an inflexible belief in the value of right and wrong, Peckinpah himself never presents this attitude as necessarily meaningful in itself; he sees it as essentially the product of an oppressive society. When Judd was a young tearaway, he was beaten up by a sheriff who wished to teach him a lesson; from this experience Judd considers he learned 'the value of self-respect'. Judd, in fact, is capable of accepting the law beyond the bounds of good sense: having saved Elsa from the Hammond brothers in the saloon, he proves ready to return her to them when he finds out that she is legally married to Billy Hammond.

Judd puts on a display of self-reliance as a defence against the world; really he is afraid of being vulnerable. This dilemma is succinctly delineated in Judd's first meeting with Gil Westrum. Judd's behaviour is that of a man who fears even to trust a friend: instead of openly accosting Westrum, Judd goes up to Westrum's rifle-range and slaps a dollar on the counter; only when Westrum proves glad to see him, does Judd abandon his masquerade as a paying customer. In the light of this gesture, Judd's offer of a job to Westrum appears a challenge to Westrum to demonstrate that he is still Judd's friend by proving worthy of Judd's trust. Judd's avowed faith in the law can be partially seen as the product of his neurotic need to control Westrum's behaviour: through his reliance on the law, Judd has ammunition both to bully Westrum into keeping the deal and to chastise him if he fails to do so.

Steve Judd is the first of the long line of Peckinpah's heroes in whom an identity crisis is defined in terms of a misalliance between puritanism and the frontier. If Judd seems at home amid the splendour of the high country – as revealed perhaps most memorably in the scene where he bathes his weary feet in a stream glinting with sunlight – there is a blackness in his heart. Indeed, the Knudsen farmstead, with its stark contrasts between scenes of sunlit pastoral and others of brooding darkness, might stand as a symbol for Judd's own psyche. In his stay at the farmstead, Judd reveals that his self-righteousness and his need to represent the law are a response to a puritan guilt. Judd is deeply oppressed by the figure of Joshua Knudsen. When at meal-time Knudsen holds forth upon man's inveterate sinfulness, Judd is the only character to take him seriously, quoting from proverbs that 'a good name is rather to be chosen than great riches, and loving favour rather than silver and gold'. On a number of occasions, Judd appears to be emotionally disturbed in a way that recalls Knudsen: at one point he even beats Heck for giving Elsa a harmless kiss. During a quiet moment together, Westrum reminds Judd of Sarah Truesdale, the woman Judd once loved and who is now married to someone else and has grandchildren. Though it is never made clear why the relationship failed, it seems likely that it may have been bound up with puritanism. Certainly Judd is now resigned to living the lonely life of a gunfighter, the loss of Sarah having been something irrevocable for him, a final severing from womankind.

'All I want is to enter my house justified' – this line of Judd's to Westrum is often quoted by critics; it was actually devised for Judd by Peckinpah's own father, who died before the film was completed. The line sums up the contradictions within Judd; it is the expression of a man trapped not just by the world but by himself. On one level, Judd's words reveal his yearning for a grand gesture that will enable him to reassert the nobility of the frontier in defiance of the debilitating effect of modern civilization. At the same time, they are the outpouring of a man who, at the mercy of the undue severity of his own conscience, nurtures within himself the desire to atone, to be punished, and is thus eternally denied true mutuality with his fellows.

Gil Westrum is one of Peckinpah's most affable characters. Unlike Judd, Westrum does not suffer from any compulsion to put principles above people. At the meal in the Knudsen home, it is Westrum who introduces a note of reality: while Knudsen and Judd exchange Biblical quotations, Westrum compliments Elsa on the meal, jestingly quoting as his reference 'Appetite: Chapter One'. Later Westrum further refutes the sermonizing of Knudsen and Judd when he calls Heck's attention to the truthfulness of a maxim on Knudsen's wall – 'When pride cometh, then cometh shame, but with the lowly cometh wisdom.' After Elsa's misguided marriage to Billy Hammond, it is Westrum who, disinclined to take the law with absolute seriousness, relieves Judge Tolliver of the marriage certificate and destroys it to free Elsa from her contract.

Yet Westrum has been corrupted by the mercenary values of town life. The gold from Coarse Gold is less than expected, but even though Westrum seems to realize that his friendship is all Judd has left in the world, he resolves to violate this friendship by making a bid for the gold. Heck, who had originally promised Westrum his help, proves reluctant in the final hour, and Westrum resorts to sophistry to persuade him to go along: 'We made a deal,' Westrum tells the boy, ignoring to mention that they have also made a deal with Judd. The attempted robbery is ingeniously handled, Peckinpah cutting between the feet of Judd and Westrum, then moving to head-and-shoulder level as Judd disarms Westrum and slaps his face. Judd tries to make Westrum draw on him but Westrum declines; disowned by Heck, Westrum realizes how badly he has let Judd down.

The attempted robbery also forces Judd to confront the limitations of his viewpoint, finally putting him in a position where he must sit in judgement on his own friend. 'My father says there's right and wrong, good and evil. It isn't that simple, is it?' Elsa tells Judd, and he sadly replies: 'No, it should be, but it isn't.' This scene between Elsa and Judd is a crucial one for an understanding of Peckinpah's work, for here Peckinpah acknowledges the intuition of a young girl above the inflexible notions of right and wrong that the Western has traditionally endorsed.

Unlike Judd, Elsa does not try to mould life in accordance with predefined values; her guiding impulse is a need to trust, and she evolves her mode of conduct in a particular situation in terms of the response this impulse elicits. Judd is inevitably drawn towards Elsa. He rushes to her defence in the Coarse Gold brothel when she stands alone wearing the white wedding dress of the dead mother her father vilifies. Elsa for Judd is the maternal principle, the heart which Judd so fears and yet so desperately needs to trust.

An encounter with the Hammonds at the Knudsen farmstead provides the occasion for a reunion between Judd and Westrum. Following a previous encounter with the Hammonds, Westrum escaped from Judd. Now he comes charging back on his horse to draw fire from Judd, Elsa and Heck, who are trapped in a ditch. Then, on Judd's instigation, Judd and Westrum take on the three surviving Hammonds in a face-off for old time's sake. The Hammonds killed, Judd is left dying, and Westrum must say a last farewell to his old friend. The last scene derives an added visual impact from what has gone before. Throughout Judd and Westrum's time on the trail together, Peckinpah has never held them side by side together in the same frame for any length of time, thus underlining the tensions that arise between them as Westrum seeks through insinuation to persuade Judd to steal the gold. But during the climactic gunfight, Peckinpah carefully frames Judd and Westrum in a two-shot as they march forward braving the Hammonds' bullets. This shot powerfully conveys how the friendship of Judd and Westrum has succeeded in triumphing against the divisive pressures that have beset it. The glory of friendship, as Judge Tolliver says of 'the glory of a good marriage', is finally seen to come through its long-term survival.

According to the conventions of the Western, Gil Westrum, in his capacity as the good-bad guy, should have been the character to die as a means of atoning for his disrespect of the law: in DeMille's *Union Pacific*, for instance,

Robert Preston's likeable outlaw finally acknowledges the necessity of the law and then dies as punishment for having conspired against the railroad. Westrum's survival constitutes the movie's final refutation of the Manicheanism of the Western. If we can speak of right and wrong, Peckinpah insists, it is not in terms of any predefined value system; rather true moral awareness can only be evolved through human contact. For Peckinpah, Westrum's claim to human dignity lies not in whether he can uphold the law but in whether he can respond to Judd's cry for friendship. Indeed, Westrum's final decision to deliver the gold to the bank in accordance with Judd's wishes is made all the more moving precisely because Westrum has not been won over to a respect for the law; he will deliver the gold solely as a last way of honouring his friend, resolutely acknowledging Judd's right to 'crash out' in his own way.

The only serious flaw in *Ride the High Country* is the character of Heck Longtree. He never becomes more than a stereotype, recalling in his final contrition the Dennis Hopper tearaways of Henry Hathaway Westerns. Heck grows blindly to accept the image of authority that Judd projects, and he is converted to lawful ways because he considers himself a bad boy. Certainly Heck hardly seems good enough for Elsa; with her awareness of life's complexity, Elsa would be better off with someone like Gil Westrum. In any case, it is difficult to imagine where Heck and Elsa can go at the end of the movie, the high country having so far been the only place which has allowed their love to grow.

Death enables the tensions in Judd to find catharsis. Judd leaves in a blaze of glory a frontier where it is no longer possible for him to live with dignity. At the same time, death provides him with a means of abdicating his position as the law: the sad beauty of his wounding derives from the fact that he is no longer setting himself up as a judge over others but accepting pain as a means of atoning to the cruel severity of his own conscience.

As he lies dying, Judd looks at the high country resplendent in its autumn colours and it seems as if the blackness no longer blights his heart; at last he is at one with the natural world around him.

> 'The regiment was like a firework that, once ignited, proceeds superior to circumstance until its blazing vitality fades.'
>
> Stephen Crane, *The Red Badge of Courage*

Major Dundee, as almost everyone who has heard of the movie knows, was mutilated by its producer. Critics usually dismiss it on these grounds as lacking in coherence. Yet *Major Dundee* remains one of Sam Peckinpah's most distinguished movies, the director's intentions still largely discernible.

Charlton Heston's Major Dundee frequently recalls the heroes Heston played for DeMille: Moses, Israel's great law-giver in *The Ten Commandments*, and the authoritarian circus boss in *The Greatest Show On Earth*. Yet whereas DeMille essentially approves of the puritan mentality; Peckinpah is of course out to criticize it. If he claims not to be a religious man, Dundee exhibits the kind of self-righteous arrogance that one associates with puritanism; 'I come to smite the wicked, not to save the heathen,' he thus excuses his forthcoming pursuit of the Apache to Reverend Dahlstrom.

Dundee is clearly practising self-delusion in the manner he unswervingly relies on the tenets of the status quo to endorse his actions. 'Whoso destroyeth my flock, I will destroy' – this dictum from Reverend Dahlstrom, the alibi under which most wars are fought, Dundee accepts totally. To Dundee the Apache are automatically in the wrong because they threaten his society and he is totally bemused when Sergeant Gomez explains to him that the Indians are on the warpath to defend their land. Dundee's faith in the law also has its limitations. Having sat at West Point on the military tribunal that cashiered Tyreen, his former friend and now prisoner, he can renounce all responsibility for the affair because 'the conscience of the court was not my concern'. Dundee also lacks political awareness. Though himself from the South, Dundee has chosen the side of the Union during the Civil War, and yet, apparently like so many of the officers of the time, he seems to have no idea what the Union stands for: indeed, although Lincoln has ostensibly claimed the emancipation of the slaves as the Unionist cause, Dundee remains fairly contemptuous of his Negro troopers.

Through Major Dundee, Peckinpah reveals the Unionist will to power as fundamentally irrational. Like so many of history's military leaders, Dundee chafes in a system to which he professes a reactionary allegiance. Relegated to spending the rest of the Civil War as a prison warden because of autocratic behaviour on the battle-field, Dundee feels compelled to define some kind of individuality by pursuing the Apache who attack the Rostes ranch. Dundee assembles a troop composed mainly of prison guards and Confederate prisoners; then, with mounts stolen by a horse thief and munitions appropriated from an army wagon-train, he sets out after the Apache. The two Rostes boys, whom the Apache abducted, are retrieved, but Dundee still does not turn back. Wreaking havoc, he carries on deeper into a Mexico under the yoke of the Austrian Emperor Maximilian and his French troops.

Possibly the most vital of *Major Dundee*'s missing scenes came at its opening. The movie, as it now stands, begins after the massacre of the Rostes ranch, but Peckinpah originally planned – and in some cases actually shot – scenes of a prison escape by Tyreen and his Southerners and their killing of a guard, of Lieutenant Brannin's cavalry troop visiting the Rostes ranch, and of the massacre of the Rostes family and the cavalry at the ranch. Presumably this would have provided us with a perspective from which to view Dundee's pursuit of the Apache, Peckinpah perhaps linking the massacre with subversive forces at the heart of the Rostes home and frontier society as a whole. Nevertheless, it remains possible to work out the significance of the Apache for Dundee as the movie goes along. Through the fears he projects on the Apache, Dundee reveals himself as afflicted by the very patriarchal society he seeks to enforce, so that the movie is very much in the tradition of American art that goes back through *The Searchers* to *Moby Dick*.

There is a distinct sexual element in Dundee's hatred of the Apache. In the early stages of the movie, Dundee's inability to cope with his own libido is evident through his narcissistic attachment to his bright blue Unionist uniform, and it eventually becomes clear that to Dundee's mind the Apache are jointly a socially acceptable target for his own libidinous drives and a surrogate for the patriarchal authority which Dundee secretly resents for preventing these drives from finding a more natural outlet. At one point, the Apache actually assume the personality of a vengeful father in their relationship to Dundee: when Dundee attempts to make love to Teresa, an Austrian doctor's widow he meets in the Mexican village, the Apache attack, 'castrating' Dundee with a wound in the leg, and condemning him henceforth to displaced aggression.

At the same time, in his fear of the Apache as 'the enemy', Dundee is unconsciously fearing the potential subversive in himself. It seems significant that the massacre in the movie's missing opening section was to be paralleled by Tyreen's escape from prison; for in Dundee's mind the Confederate captain clearly is linked with the Apache, Peckinpah suggesting that the Union's desire to combat the South partially had its origins in a puritan desire to control subversive elements. To Dundee Tyreen is a 'traitor' and a 'murderer'; and when Dundee attacks the Confederate Captain in an explosion of anger, he appears to be hitting out at the subversive in himself since he himself is originally of Southern birth. Thus, when Dundee uses the threat of hanging to compel Tyreen and his men to join in the Indian pursuit, he is in his mind forcing one insurrectionary phantom to control another insurrectionary phantom.

Captain Ben Tyreen, too, is a man of contradictions. He can carry honour to absurd extremes; he even kills one of his own men for deserting Dundee because he himself has given his word to Dundee that the South will continue pursuit 'until the Apache are taken or destroyed'. Before the Civil War, Tyreen has ridden with Grant, and he has only sided with the South after being cashiered from West Point for 'a duel of honour'; indeed, in the civility he shows to the Negroes, Tyreen contrasts both with the Southerners he commands and with Dundee. Thus, as Dundee is driven to sock Tyreen, Tyreen is driven to sock Dundee, at once hitting out against a status quo he despises and the Northerner he needs to suppress in himself.

Yet Tyreen is a far more attractive character than Dundee. If Dundee acts as the mindless agent of a dominant culture, Tyreen, driven to reject totally such a culture ('I would rather hang than serve'), lays claim to being something more than a cipher in a historical process. Tyreen's overriding motivation appears to be frustration with everything. Doubtless, this frustration would have appeared all the more desperate if the movie's producer had permitted us to see Tyreen's abortive escape attempt. As it is, however, there remain moments when this frustration takes on a metaphysical power. In one extraordinary scene during the prison sequence, Tyreen, at once a Christ and newly fallen Satan, stands with his manacled arms outstretched while shadows flung by prison bars fall on his frame like fetters upon his very soul.

The man of the South has always been a figure of escape and revolt in American cinema. For instance, there is the trooper Tyree of Ford's cavalry movies: Tyree is a man who likes to spend most of his time on lone patrols; and, at the end of *Rio Grande*, he rides away into the hills, pursued by the law, while his Union commander is left to brave the confusions of marriage and army red tape. Peckinpah's Tyreen, however, is a more darkly romantic figure than is perhaps usual for the man of the South. At times, Tyreen recalls the Errol Flynn of Raoul Walsh; during the sequence of the Mexican fiesta, he even demonstrates a Flynn-like sword thrust to Dundee. Like Flynn's Custer in *They Died With Their Boots On*, Tyreen is driven on by a love of death. Of all the men who pursue the Apache, he is the one who most indelibly appears to be pursuing a mental image. As Dundee's troop crosses the Rio Grande into Mexico, Tyreen sights a troop of Confederate cavalry. He feels driven to break his oath to Dundee, not so much because of any sympathy with the South, but because death and glory beckon – or so we feel since in the indistinct distance the horsemen appear like some ghostly vision. In the movie's climactic battle between Dundee's troop and French lancers, Tyreen is severely wounded. Looking about him, he sights a line of French lancers charging in the distance. As with the Confederate cavalry earlier, these horsemen have a ghostly aura. This time, however, Tyreen charges forth, dying in a terrain that for him is suffused with his own inner dream reality.

'Until the Apache are taken or destroyed.' *Major Dundee* examines how a new nation can define a blanket identity through an act of external aggression, the men who accompany Dundee in his pursuit having various motives for their complicity. Like their commander, some are plagued by sexual terrors – they can only alleviate that through aggression against some external force: Bugler Ryan is prompted to enlist by the spectacle of the ravished corpse of Beth Rostes, a girl with whom he was having a presumably chaste relationship; while Reverend Dahlstrom joins to avenge the violation of the Rostes' marriage, a union he himself had sanctified. Samuel Potts, the scout, has a great affinity with the Indians, yet he goes along with Dundee to exterminate them and the only way of life that is congenial to himself because, a warrior by nature, this is the only means left for him to exercise his abilities. With his primitive morality, Potts proves the ideal aid to Dundee; 'The Major ain't no lawyer,' he warns French troops who insist Dundee has no right to 'liberate' from them a Mexican village and its supply of food. In one scene, Potts challenges Riago, his Indian companion, to a bout of wrestling. The bout provides Potts with a means of demonstrating that, despite having only one arm, he is as good a man as any. At the same time, Potts here recalls Dundee and Tyreen with their blows at one another; for, in grappling with Riago, Potts is attacking an aspect of his own personality that threatens the type of society he has come to accept.

Peckinpah takes an obvious delight in the various national and racial types that compose Dundee's detachment, mourning the manner in which true identities can be swamped beneath the emergence of America as a modern state. Sergeant Gomez is a Mexican who has ridden with the Indians (though the latter is no longer clear thanks to the producer's cuts) and he seems to have taken the job of soldier as a facile way out of an identity dilemma. Riago, Potts' Indian friend, is a Christian Indian and has thus been bound through the misguided zeal of missionaries to fight against his own kind. Throughout the movie, Riago, for all his pains, only ever meets with jibes and insults from Dundee and most of the company. The Southern prisoners go along with Dundee because of their allegiance to Tyreen and because of Dundee's promise that after the pursuit he will let them go home. This promise, however, is meaningless; after the pursuit, the war will probably be over and they will have no home left. The Negro troopers, tired of cleaning stables, go with Dundee because they wish to assert a claim to dignity by earning the white-man's praise. However, most of them end up shot to pieces and hardly anyone ever seems to notice they are around. *Major Dundee* seems ahead of its time in its implication that the blackman might do better to act in accordance with standards he himself has evolved; Robert Aldrich's *Apache* is the only Western made before it, as far as I recall, that does as near as much violence to the Hollywood stereotype of the Negro as noble slave.

In the first part of *Major Dundee*, Peckinpah examines how an officer can maintain a credibility before those he commands by remaining aloof from them. When Dundee is first seen in the film as it now stands, he is posed statuesquely in one corner of the frame, ordering his men past him towards the Rostes ranch. At the prison, Dundee is seen mostly seated behind his desk, on the balcony outside his office or on high points around the prison. Only in the few instances when he makes any direct contact with the men does Dundee's authority appear precarious.

Peckinpah is dismayed at the manner military discipline can induce a peculiar mental blankness in the individual soldier. During a scene where Captain Waller questions Dundee's motives in pursuing the Apache, Peckinpah keeps cutting to Sergeant Gomez, who, standing stiffly to attention in the same room, appears to have no interest at all in a conversation that will decide his own fate. Bugler Ryan is the movie's narrator; his diary, a voice at the opening tells us, provides history's only record of Dundee's campaign against the Apache. Ryan's narration often conceals or misrepresents the truth: Ryan calls Teresa German when we know she is Austrian, and, on a more serious level, he dismisses the vicious bout of wrestling between Potts and Riago as a 'friendly contest'. 'If Lieutenant Brannin were still alive he would have hung Riago and I would have helped,' Ryan, early on in the movie, informs us on the subject of Potts' Indian friend, who is mistakenly suspected of complicity in the massacre at the Rostes ranch. The unquestioning obedience Ryan felt for Brannin, he readily transfers to Dundee. Later Peckinpah has Ryan, like Gomez, standing to attention during one of Dundee's interviews, in this instance between Dundee and Potts. As Potts defends Riago to Dundee, Ryan remains totally heedless of the defence, seemingly accepting the Major's suspicions of the Indian as founded. Through Ryan's narration, *Major Dundee* becomes a critique of the awe for authority with which history has been presented in the Western in general, Peckinpah forcing his audience to distinguish between what seems and what is in a way that Dundee's soldiers never do.

As the movie progresses, the image Dundee seeks to project is forced to disintegrate. The pursuit of the Apache turns out to be less glorious than Dundee anticipated. The Apache attack from ambush as the company patrol a river at night. The ambush is shot mostly in pans to register Dundee's confusion; and since Peckinpah uses a similar technique in an earlier scene where, watched by a grinning Dundee, Lieutenant Graham seeks to control stampeding horses in the prison compound, the ambush makes Dundee appear to be assuming the qualities of clumsiness and awkwardness which so amused him in Graham. The ambush is followed by a mass burial of dead soldiers to 'Gather at the river', a scene of bitter irony.

Dundee's image is undermined further when during the sojourn at the Mexican village, he is exposed to a woman for the first time in the film. When

Dundee meets Teresa, he is driven, despite himself, quietly to distraction after he glimpses a naked area of her bosom as she crosses her shawl. Dundee's rank, although he makes a display of it to her, means nothing to Teresa; at the fiesta, she is as glad to dance with Lieutenant Graham as she is with Dundee. Yet she is finally drawn to Dundee by a need to show him kindness. After the fiesta, Dundee and Teresa meet alone in the Daliesque landscape of a broken arch in a twilight setting. But even now Dundee cannot relax and feels compelled to assert his superiority to others; 'He is corrupt but I will save him', Dundee proclaims of Lieutenant Graham, obviously still resenting that Graham danced with Teresa.

The execution of O.W.Hadley, one of Tyreen's men, is central to the movie's moral concerns. The scene takes place in a paradisal riverside setting where Teresa has been reunited with Dundee, having fled the village after the French have razed it. Hadley has been captured after stealing supplies and deserting and everyone waits to see what the Major will do. Tyreen agreeing with him, Hadley claims he has gone over the hill before and always come back. When Hadley claims he deserted for a woman, Dundee and Teresa exchange glances, Dundee seeming to acknowledge a complicity with Hadley. Yet Dundee still condemns Hadley to death because this is what the book says. Tyreen shoots Hadley rather than let someone else do it, swearing revenge on Dundee when the pursuit is over. 'Hell, Major, you're just doing what you have to do, but damn your soul for it!' – Hadley's final words express at once a resentment for the tyranny of the rule-book and an acceptance that such a tyranny must be, thus summing up the tragedy of the situation that the scene depicts.

As with Steve Judd, it is when he must sit in judgement on another that Dundee is finally forced to confront the limitations of the law he seeks to uphold. Yet Dundee alone is not to blame for the tragedy: so are the soldiers and Mexicans who stand around in mute compliance, only Tyreen raising a muddled protest. Authoritarianism, Peckinpah seems to be saying, is something that the individual must reject as it exists both outside of himself and within his own personality; only then can people acknowledge a common humanity. Thanks to an honest and open affair with a Mexican girl, Ryan by this point has developed some kind of individuality, and his narration lends a final note of hope to the scene. 'But he bears the burden of command and I do not feel fit to judge him' – finally Ryan is able to look at Dundee and recognize just another human being.

Dundee then abandons himself to desires similar to those for which he has had Hadley killed. In flight from himself, he wanders along the riverside with Teresa. The two of them briefly seem to feel at home with the natural splendour around them. 'Are you *el tigre*, the tiger who prowls the mountains?' Teresa asks Dundee; and it is as if she is asking him to accept those forces in his personality he is out to repress in his pursuit of the Apache. Dundee is moved by Teresa's show of love for him and bathes himself in the river with her, thus symbolically shedding his repressive conscience. When they return to the river bank, Dundee, for the first time in the movie, is able to reflect on how the army really works, musing about how fighting on an officer's orders provides men with an easy way of escaping from their problems and responsibilities. 'But who do you answer to?' Teresa asks Dundee, and she receives her reply in the form of an Apache arrow that hits Dundee in the leg and brings their idyll to an end; Dundee's repressive conscience has returned with a vengeance. Soon, Tyreen is standing over Dundee like a further extension of this conscience, upbraiding the Major for leaving his post to consort with a woman of 'easy virtue'.

Peckinpah exposes the essential masochism by which a figure of authority functions, Dundee as much the prisoner of the image he projects of himself as his men are of it. Having made a slip, Dundee cannot live with himself and discards his uniform for rags to seek drunken oblivion in the Mexican town of Durango. Dundee's relationship with Teresa disintegrates as she leaves to fight with revolutionaries against the French and he takes to whoring in an attempt to forget his impotence towards her. When Tyreen and a detachment from the company, now held together by Graham, arrive in Durango, they find Dundee lying in a gutter, a mongrel licking his face. Tyreen explains to Dundee how he, too, hates the parts he has played in life – Irish potato farmer, cashiered Union officer, Confederate renegade – and the two men lash out at one another, this time their blows coming as an acknowledgement that they are brothers in self-disgust. For all its repressive force, the wounding enables Dundee to discover a solidarity with his men; it brings home to him that he is not all-powerful but a vulnerable human being like everyone else.

As we might expect of a man who is resolutely proud of his own Indian extraction, Peckinpah originally planned for Dundee's company to be wiped out without catching the Apache: 'It was important for the meaning of the film that Dundee did not catch the Indian Charriba because I wanted to show that the quest was an end in itself.' This would have been in keeping with how the Apache increase in grandeur during the movie, finally representing as magnificent those forces that their pursuers and American civilization are out to destroy. But this ending was not to be, Peckinpah's producer insisting that the Indians must die. Dundee's victory over the Indians is shot by Peckinpah in a deliberately unspectacular manner; Sierra Charriba, the Indian chief, is killed by Bugler Ryan and then hurled like a dog into a ditch with other corpses. In Charriba's death, as so often with death in Peckinpah's movies, we are reminded of the Westerns of Budd Boetticher; as after a Boetticher gunfight, we feel profound sadness that a contest is over.

It is something of a convention in the American cinema that films about war celebrate energy. But in *Major Dundee* this celebration is charged with a singular defiance. Dundee's company finally driven on by frenzy, we see in the closing stages of the movie something akin to the mad Fredonia of which Turk in *The Deadly Companions* fantasized. The movie's climax is now provided by a fight with French lancers ('a real war'), which, edited in a blow for blow manner, builds up to a tremendous crescendo. The French, mindless imperialists, remind us of what Dundee initially sought to make of his men. Now Dundee's company, bedraggled and used to fighting with guerrilla tactics, are more like the Indians than the French. Thus, their wreaking of havoc among the French comes as an expression of their final refusal to be coerced by the military ethic. 'Only thunderbolts can be preferred to cannon', Graham, quoting Napoleon, is in the habit of boasting on the subject of the company's howitzer, and in the climactic battle this gun comes to stand for the explosive dynamism of the company itself as Graham uses it to blast away at the French, having previously briefly tried it out against them on Dundee's entry into the Mexican village.

The battle ends with Tyreen's death. Tyreen is wounded saving the company's colours and these he gives to Dundee before riding forth against a line of French lancers. The image of Dundee brandishing the American flag is of importance of our understanding of the final development of the Major's character. At the beginning of the movie, the American flag, seen at various places in the prison, is a tangible symbol for Dundee's authority. Later, the significance of the flag changes. Dundee has the company's colours concealed during his entry into the Mexican village, a fact remarked by Teresa, and also refuses to let them be shown after his wounding at the riverside. Thus, the sight of Dundee no longer afraid to show the flag in the final battle suggests that the Major has attained some capacity to accept responsibility for his actions. At the same time, since the concealment of the flag is linked to Dundee's final impotence towards Teresa, this image suggests that Dundee's libido is making a delayed claim to some form of potency by discharging itself through violence. It is fitting also that it is Tyreen who should restore the flag to Dundee since in Tyreen's subsequent death, watched by Dundee, the violent forces driving the company are at once affirmed and atoned for.

That the producer did not allow Peckinpah to finally have Dundee's whole company wiped out is also unfortunate since Dundee should find death to complete his moral development: after finally squaring up against a nightmare father through violence, he needs, like Steve Judd, to meet death as a means of atonement and thus irrevocably abdicate his position as law-giver. As it is, the movie now ends on a note of complete bitterness. Major Dundee, initially committed to the Union as a unificatory force, finally becomes himself the embodiment of a nation that refuses to be integrated; if Dundee is probably eternally damned to be at war with himself, the very existence of this war within him is evidence of his continuing vitality as a human being. We never learn whether the army brass court-martial Dundee or make him a hero for his actions: but, however they will rationalize the campaign, we feel sure that they will never be able to understand how so many men could have finally fought and died just for the hell of it rather than to uphold any of the values of American civilization. As Sam Peckinpah says of the end of the movie: 'It was written and shot so that the battle – even though Sierra Charriba was dead – would never end; it hasn't yet.'

A Note of Mourning For *The Glory Guys*

An even greater example of Hollywood's lack of imagination than the studio's butchering of Major Dundee is the fate of *The Glory Guys*, which Peckinpah scripted but was not allowed to direct.

Peckinpah wrote the screenplay to stave off financial difficulty when he was out of work after *Major Dundee*. The movie was produced in a ridiculous manner. Demas Harrod, a cavalry captain, and Sol Rogers, an Indian scout, are both men supposed to be getting on in years, yet the actors who play them do not look much above thirty; while Senta Berger is the last person one would imagine to play Lou Woodward, a middle-aged frontier widow. Arnold Laven's direction is totally unimaginative: the Indians all look like 'make-believe' Indians from the rodeo procession in Peckinpah's own *Junior Bonner*; and a river beside which the scout finally meets his death appears as little more than a muddy stream – one can imagine the paradisal beauty Peckinpah would have injected into this setting if only he had been allowed to direct the movie. It says a great deal for Peckinpah's artistic integrity that, given the lack of artistry involved in the production, he bothered to produce a script of some distinction. Thus, the movie is of interest here because it contains, if these are hardly developed, a number of characteristic Peckinpah preoccupations.

Peckinpah's script depicts cavalry life with a bitterness that is unusual for Westerns made at that time. The movie begins by introducing us to the new recruits of a cavalry platoon; these are drifters, unemployed immigrants and a young boy out to escape an unjust shotgun wedding. The men learn that General McCabe, who commands their company, is obsessed with glory and that they will most likely all end up sacrificed to his mad schemes; and the rest of the movie details how, despite their knowledge of this, these men are welded into a fighting force, Peckinpah out to examine perhaps even more fully than in *Major Dundee* how the army seeks to break down a man's personality and replace it by another. During training, the platoon are taken out for a ride and attacked by other soldiers dressed as Indians. From the fury and madness with which they respond to their fake attackers, they reveal the mindlessness with which recruits can be made to see an opposing force as 'the enemy'.

The platoon discover a common fellowship: when some of them are embroiled in a saloon brawl, the rest break orders to rescue them. Yet in the overall context of the theatre of war such devotion is seen sadly to enforce the status quo of the Union. In yet another potentially marvellous scene, a soldier blows his top while firing at Indians and fails to obey an order to retreat. His friend refuses to leave him; and when the soldier is killed, the friend stands alone facing a line of charging Indians – it is a heroic but futile death.

In many ways, the platoon's desire to fight the Indians seems prompted by a need to channel aggressions that spring from a resentment of their officers. Peckinpah seems to share this resentment. During a ball, the snobbery of the officer class is made clear when General McCabe's wife insults the widow, Lou Woodward, because she feels the widow lacks propriety in her personal life. The widow begins to cry and everyone except Captain Harrod ignores her tears. Such a class, it seems, can blindly trust their generals and politicians and yet feel able to pass judgement on another person's private life.

Like *Major Dundee*, the movie is punctuated by fist fights. Harrod and the Indian scout both pay court to the widow, but put more effort into fighting one another than into their courtship. Harrod is obsessed by death; and although he realizes McCabe is unhinged, he goes along with him on a campaign against the Indians because it provides an escape for him from his anxieties about relating to the widow: 'Don't wait for me; I won't be back', he tells the widow before he rides away. But it is the scout and not Harrod who is killed in the final battle when most of McCabe's company are massacred. Finally confronted with the full meaninglessness of death, Harrod begins to ponder upon the true beauty of life. It is possible that he might really be able to love the widow when he returns to the fort. *The Glory Guys*, it seems, would have provided as penetrating a study as *Major Dundee* of the sexual undertones of the American cinema's preoccupation with the journey to war.

> 'The slave revolt in morals begins by rancour turning creative and giving birth to values – the rancour of beings who, deprived of the direct outlet of action, compensate by an imaginary vengeance. All truly noble morality grows out of triumphant self-affirmation.'
>
> Friedrich Nietzsche, *The Genealogy of Morals*

So many American movies deal with heroes who meet with violent deaths, but perhaps no movie has more claim than Peckinpah's *The Wild Bunch* to the title of the American cinema's greatest hymn to 'crashing out'. Born into a world beset by the deluded rationalizations of puritanism and totalitarianism, sons of a tyrannical, law-giving father and a mother that never showed them love, the outlaws that comprise the Wild Bunch are men driven on by pain and confusion; their only satisfaction is that of making a last defiant gesture of disaffiliation before they, like the rest of their breed, are wiped off the face of the earth forever.

At the head of the Wild Bunch is Pike Bishop, perhaps the most contradiction-ridden of all Peckinpah's contradiction-ridden heroes. In some respects Bishop responds with pragmatism to the world in which he lives, an America that has entered the First World War. He can sacrifice his men for the survival of the Bunch: during a bank robbery, he leaves Crazy Lee behind to die taking care of hostages; then he shoots Buck, who is blinded and unable to travel; later he abandons Sykes when the old man has been picked off by a posse. Yet, at the same time, Bishop still remains attached to old ideals: he weeps inside because, during an ambush by the law, he escaped and left behind Deke Thornton, then his friend, to be captured.

Under his calm exterior, Bishop is cracking up. At times his actions have a crazy bravado that overlays a desire for death: when, for instance, Bishop threatens to blow up himself and the Bunch with a wagon-load of ammunition if *federales* come any closer, the suspense is tremendous because we *know* Bishop would carry out his threat. Like *White Heat*, *The Wild Bunch* derives much of its suspense from our knowledge of the hero's impending madness.

A scene early in the movie illustrates how Bishop musters a stern resolve to mask his basic vulnerability. His horse having floundered in desert sand, Bishop attempts to remount but falls to the ground in pain when his stirrup-strap snaps. Amid laughter and taunts from the Gorch brothers, he finally makes it into the saddle and rides on proudly, Peckinpah's camera lingering upon his lonely and isolated figure as he heads into the distance. Later, Bishop tells Dutch, his confidant in the Bunch, that the painful leg wound is the price he paid for once having loved a woman. This incident is told in flashback. The woman is Mexican and married. She slaps Bishop for being late. As she strips off and they prepare to make love, we see reflected in a mirror the image of some dark avenger who stands in the doorway to the room. The woman's husband has arrived: shots ring out, leaving the woman dead and Bishop wounded. Each day of his life, Bishop tells Dutch, he dreams of catching up with the assassin. This memory has all the resonances of an Oedipal drama: a forbidding slap from a woman and punishment when sex is dared.

Another flashback explains Bishop's past friendship with Deke Thornton. Although Thornton has consented to lead a posse after him as payment for being freed from prison, Bishop still thinks of him as a friend; and as Bishop and Dutch turn in on the trail, Bishop's mind goes back to the time he and Thornton were ambushed. The flashback shows them in a brothel together. Recalling the Hammonds in *Ride the High Country*, the two men are sharing women. Playing the role of a protective older brother to Thornton, Bishop assures him that they are safe from the law. But, as in the scene with the Mexican woman, a moment of repose is shattered: men arrive with guns and Bishop flees for his life, forced to abandon Thornton.

For the framework to this flashback Peckinpah keeps cutting from Bishop to Thornton further back along the trail, underlining the bond that exists between the two men by making them appear to have the same memory. This cutting also indicates a gulf between Bishop and Dutch. When Dutch suggests to Bishop that the next time around they may not have a chance, Bishop replies, 'I wouldn't have it any other way.' Dutch is not alarmed by the fascination with death evident in Bishop's words. 'I wouldn't have it any other way, either', he says, his voice filled with emotion, then turns over and goes to sleep. Still reflecting on Thornton, Bishop is unable to perceive Dutch's own loyalty.

Bishop's ambivalence towards women provides us with a key to an understanding of his affection for Thornton. It is no mere coincidence that Bishop should express a desire for death as he thinks of Thornton. It is clear that Thornton has become a target for the libido Bishop can no longer direct towards women. Bishop's longing for Thornton manifests itself in his growing passivity towards him. Twice during the movie – in the opening bank raid and following the raid on the ammunition train – Bishop finds himself in Thornton's gunsights and remains poised there as if unconsciously yearning for Thornton's bullet to penetrate his body.

The members of the Bunch who survive the opening bank robbery with Bishop recall their leader in various ways. Dutch, filled with contempt for all custodians of authority, sticks with Bishop partly in the hope of some day being able to square off against such authority. Delighting in sharing whores, the Gorch brothers remind us of how the friendship between Bishop and Thornton was. More than the other members of the Bunch, the Gorches are men for whom the gun provides the most natural means of expression: even during their orgy amid wine-vats, they brandish their guns, blasting away at the vats. Yet there is a despair about the two men: Lyle introduces one of the Mexican whores from the orgy to Bishop as his fiancée, seeking to constitute in drunkenness a security he can never know in life. The other surviving member of the Bunch is Angel, a young Mexican psychopath, driven to the Bunch as a reaction against a home country beset by dictators. In Angel the full tragedy of the Bunch's misogyny is made clear. Angel's wife, Teresa, whom he regards as a goddess, becomes the whore of the Mexican dictator, Mapache. When the Bunch visit Mapache's camp, Angel meets Teresa again. She recognizes him and struggles to suppress tears – perhaps she still loves him. But then she turns to Mapache, putting on a smile. Angel is unable even to contemplate whether she still loves him: he can only cut himself off from a possible source of love. When he sees Teresa embrace Mapache, he explodes and guns her down.

The Marquis de Sade once wrote: 'To kill a man in a paroxysm of passion is understandable. To have him killed by someone else after serious meditation and on the pretext of a duty honourably discharged is incomprehensible.' By this token we do not hate Angel when he murders his wife: he is acting in a state of painful confusion and would never claim any moral justification for his action. In contrast to Angel stand the mass-murderers: Harrigan, Thornton's big boss, who can bring about the destruction of a town because 'we represent the law', and Mapache, who callously takes and sacrifices lives in the name of his power as dictator.

Throughout the movie, the Wild Bunch derive a kind of dignity from the way their actions appear to spring from an inability to renounce pain. In the opening bank robbery, the explosive wildness of the Bunch cuts through the hypocrisy of the town of Starbuck. This sequence begins with a shot of scorpions amid killer ants. The image provides a metaphor for the Bunch's relationship to the society through which they move, and it presents a world where instincts reign. Over a subsequent shot of the insects, the Temperance Union of Starbuck are heard taking an oath to stamp out drinking, thus suggesting civilization's hostility to the instinct world. Lying on a rooftop with Thornton and bounty hunters, Harrigan presides over the Bunch's arrival in soldiers' garb, while the matrons of the Temperance Union, accompanied by men in eastern suits, parade down the main street. If the Temperance Union's singing of 'Gather at the river' reminds us of *My Darling Clementine*, this is by no means fortuitous; we are watching again the scene of Wyatt Earp and Clementine's walk to the half-built church, only this time it is shot without any sleight of hand so that it becomes an unequivocal celebration of masculine frustrations. As the Wild Bunch charge from the bank with their loot, they tear into the Temperance Union like a defiant resurgence of the libido, a slow-motion effusion of violence beginning; and, left inside the bank to hold up the rear, Crazy Lee forces hostages to join him in singing a mocking reprise of 'Gather at the river'.

Early in the gun battle, Peckinpah establishes the Bunch's aggression as a consequence of frustrated heterosexual union. He frames a little boy and girl tentatively seeking to embrace in the middle of the main street, threatened on all sides by violence. Then he links two boys near the comparative safety of a building with Bishop and Dutch escaping together, thus suggesting the durable power of the male bond. Heterosexual disharmony becomes the keynote of the battle as, by aggression against the demure womanhood of Starbuck, the Wild Bunch define a spontaneous refusal to accept integration. Inside the bank, Crazy Lee takes a particular fancy to a haughty woman who calls him 'trash' and he proceeds to force his attentions upon her. In the main street, careering horses become symbols for the unbridled and uncontrollable fury of the group: Bishop rides down a woman as he escapes and another of the Bunch crashes into a shop window on his horse, scattering mannequins decked in women's finery.

Finally, the holocaust comes to a close: as Crazy Lee makes a mad last stand against Harrigan's men, and the remnants of the Bunch make it to the outskirts of town, as if spewed forth by a civilization that finds it impossible to digest them.

Finding themselves penniless when their loot turns out to be washers planted by Harrigan, the Bunch head for Mexico in search of more action. There they spend a brief sojourn at Angel's village. The whole sequence is suffused with nostalgia. In contrast to the spectre of the vengeful father who torments the Bunch, the village elder is more concerned to understand people than to judge them. 'We all dream of being a child again, the worst of us most of all', the elder tells Bishop. 'You know what we are then,' Bishop replies, finally feeling he can relax. Even the Gorch brothers relax their violence, gently courting a Mexican girl. As Bishop, Sykes and the elder begin to laugh, Peckinpah cuts to a *fiesta* as if this is a natural extension of their good humour. The cut to the *fiesta*, however, is also overlaid with Angel's wail of 'where is Mapache?' The spectre of the cruel father haunts the Bunch even in this Eden, for Angel craves revenge on Mapache for having taken his wife and killed his father. As the Wild Bunch leave, villagers line their path to bid farewell, and it is as if they perceive an aura of death about the outlaws.

Despite their affection for the Mexican villagers, the Wild Bunch appear to feel little sympathy for the revolutionaries who fight Mapache. Meeting up with Mapache, the Bunch take on the job of robbing an American munitions train for him. As the Bunch pick up payment for the robbery, Mapache takes Angel prisoner, having learned that Angel has given one box of rifles to the revolutionaries. Angel's capture is one of Peckinpah's most moving scenes. Dutch, who has accompanied Angel into Mapache's camp to pick up payment for the robbery, has no alternative but to disown Angel and ride away. Angel looks after him sadly; having saved Dutch's life during the train robbery, he feels Dutch is now betraying his friendship. Among the mocking faces about him, Angel searches for one that is not hostile; realizing he is finished, he fights to stifle tears.

Angel's capture provides a nexus point for many of the key themes and *motifs* of the movie. Zooms and pans characterize the movie's style, the general effect being of tableaux capsizing into chaos; and Angel's capture is accompanied by chaotic pans around mocking faces, expressing total disorientation. Angel's capture also relates to the movie's *motif* of the powerlessness of an individual or individuals to avert disaster. The American officer who realizes too late that his company is involved in a train crash, the Bunch reacting too late to prevent Angel from killing his wife and to prevent Mapache from killing Angel – these are other instances of the same *motif*. Angel's cruel fate also provides a metaphor for the psychological anguish that torments the Bunch. The duty-bound soldier is a familiar figure both in America and in Mapache's Mexico: on the munitions train, we see young American army recruits who, soon to be plunged into war in Europe, remain unable to question their fate; and in Mapache's camp, the behaviour of the soldiers is characterized by total subservience – at one point a young soldier mutely accepts death for having fired overhastily on the Bunch. Like Harrigan, Mapache is associated with the suppression of the maternal principle. The Temperance Union back up Harrigan's authority in Starbuck, and most of the women in Mapache's camp appear the exclusive possessions of Mapache and his officer *élite;* it is in a gesture of contempt that Mapache casts three of his less attractive women to the Gorch brothers. Angel's fate at Mapache's hands thus stands for the fate of the individual before patriarchal oppression. Since he is betrayed by Teresa's mother ('His own momma turned him in', Lyle Gorch says of this), Angel appears like a son betrayed by his own mother. Eventually butchered by Mapache, Angel becomes the son killed by the father who sired him but who could not let him live.

'When you side with a man, you stick with him. If you can't do that you're worse than some animal.' When Pike Bishop says these words, he is secretly brooding upon his own abandonment of Deke Thornton. With time, these words become a maxim for the Bunch. Even the Gorch brothers begin to display solidarity; after the train robbery, Tector Gorch shares his whiskey with his comrades; and Lyle Gorch, once so resentful of Angel, is shocked when he hears that Angel is Mapache's prisoner. Having made enough money to live comfortably, the Bunch decide that is not enough: they also want dignity. Seeing Angel tortured, Bishop decides it is time that he himself atoned for his abandonment of Thornton: 'Let's go', he makes his familiar call to action one more time, and the four men fill the frame as they walk together through Mapache's camp; appropriately, a brief two-shot of Dutch and Bishop reminds us of Westrum and Judd's last walk in *Ride the High Country*. On the soundtrack can be heard the Mexican chant, now sung drunkenly, with which the Bunch were serenaded as they left Angel's village. But the Bunch cannot save Angel; in a grim joke, Mapache slits his throat before their eyes. Now the Bunch must go ahead and fight – a gesture which becomes a final outcry against all of the forces oppressing them.

Angel's tortured figure being dragged around behind Mapache's shiny red car links Mapache's cruelty with the notion of the inhumanness of modern technology. The Wild Bunch's last stand is partly a reaction against this inhumanness. Grabbing Mapache's machine gun, they blast away at his soldiers; like Mark Twain's Connecticut Yankee, they use modern weaponry to express a total disenchantment with technological progress. Their stand is an affirmation of the claims of the instinct world, of the frontier which civilization has outlawed and yet not made fully extinct. Indeed, Mapache's slitting of Angel's throat seems more to arouse the Bunch physically rather than outrage them morally; it makes them explode with that savage fury which Jack London called 'the ecstasy that marks the summit of life'. Prefigured by the drunken revelry of Mapache and his officers, the final massacre, with its lingering slow-motion deaths, becomes an orgiastic experience; in fact, in its sound effects of gunfire and women's screams, it reminds us of the Gorch brothers' orgy amid the wine-vats.

A major factor behind the irrationality of the Wild Bunch's last stand is sexual frustration. Having now made it rich, they have no alternative but to confront their essential unhappiness. This is made clear in a scene that prefigures their march to confront Mapache. Pike Bishop is desperately sad as he spends time with a young Mexican girl. We have seen her eyeing Bishop earlier; then the possibility of her getting to know him was forestalled by Angel's killing of his wife. Though she has given herself to him not as a prostitute, Bishop still insists on giving her money, and it seems likely that his gesture is an attempt to compensate for some sexual failure towards her. Besides locating Bishop's last stand as a reaction against fears of sexual impotence, the scene also presents his love of death in terms of a yearning for maternal ground. As Bishop looks at the girl, his face is overlain with the noise of her baby crying, and he appears not as her lover, but as a son who waits for just one sign of affection from his mother to relieve the coldness of being outside the womb. Abandoning himself as much to the impulse to live out his inner drama of pain into madness as a wish to save Angel, Bishop steps into the next room where the Gorch brothers argue about money with a whore they have shared. They, too, have had enough: to Bishop's call of 'Let's go', Lyle Gorch replies 'Why not?', an acknowledgement of desperation shared.

The final showdown begins when the Wild Bunch gun down Mapache after he has slit Angel's throat. A brief silence follows, then Pike Bishop shoots

Mapache's authoritarian German adviser. At this, Mapache's troops hurl themselves at the Bunch in a mad rush; it is as if they fear some contagion from the Bunch's actions might spread into themselves. By taking hold of the machine-gun, the Bunch assume the role of a manic travesty of the father, since the machine-gun can be seen subliminally as a symbol for Mapache's power. Since all Mapache's women die in the holocaust, the Bunch in their suicidal stand also express their misogyny; Dutch is even seen holding a woman against himself, using her as a shield against bullets.

When, in the heat of the battle, Bishop steps into a room which appears empty except for himself and a Mexican woman, he appears to be stepping into the past, to that night of the dark avenger. One of Peckinpah's most bizarre moments ensues. Bishop fires into a mirror that reflects the woman's image, and his shot kills a man who is suddenly revealed to be lurking behind the mirror; perhaps at last Bishop has really caught up with the avenger. Refusing to see the woman as a threat, Bishop turns his back on her to fire at troops in the yard outside. But the woman, virago-like, shoots Bishop in the back: woman has affirmed her identity as betrayer. 'Bitch!' – Bishop turns on the woman and guns her down, as if revenging himself on the whole of womankind. This exchange of gunfire has *Liebestod* connotations of forbidden passions discharging themselves, for soon afterwards Bishop finds the death for which he has yearned for so long. The Gorch brothers have already died orgasmically at the machine-gun, and when Bishop himself takes hold of the gun, the floodgates of love open up in his personality. If through death Bishop is atoning for a parricidal guilt, he also demonstrates how the human psyche can stay human despite the workings of a repressive conscience; it is as if each bullet fired into him comes not from Mapache's soldiers but from Deke Thornton. Bishop's death finally becomes a tribute to the invincibility of Eros, the outlaw leader attaining the orgasm that has been denied him with woman. But a note of sadness is introduced by the figure of Dutch, making his way to Bishop's side to die there; Bishop, close to death, is even now unable to appreciate his friend's loyalty. Once again, we are reminded of the solitude with which Bishop was forced to live out his last days on earth.

The battle ends. Deke Thornton and his bounty hunters move in. Throughout the movie, Thornton has revealed a loving admiration towards Pike Bishop akin to that of Ford's Wyatt Earp for his Doc Holliday; and, as Tyreen's mad charge did for Major Dundee, the spectacle of Bishop's death has helped Thornton resolve a conflict in himself. When Thornton affectionately takes Bishop's gun, he is not only professing respect for his outlaw friend; he is also affirming an allegiance to forces in his own personality which he would have to suppress in order to adapt to Harrigan's America. With Bishop dead, Thornton can go back across the border, yet he has no inclination to do so. When old Sykes appears with revolutionaries, Thornton decides to go along with them.

Through Thornton, Bishop's gun can find a fitting home: wielded and abandoned in a struggle against a nightmare father, it has been purged of its insane fearsomeness; it can now be used to build rather than tear down. The Wild Bunch's drama of pain over, it seems possible for men to be bound together by a common brotherhood.

To end his movie, Peckinpah presents a reprise of the Wild Bunch laughing, culled from earlier scenes in the movie; they appear at last cleansed from fear. 'By ending with these killers as they laugh, behaving as everyone does,' Peckinpah says of his ending, 'I wanted to remind the audience that they were just people like themselves.' Perhaps by the same token, Peckinpah also intended his audience to acknowledge in the Bunch a more familiar image of themselves – that of a humanity blasted by pain and committed to liberation from the depths of its being.

> 'Supposing that I should have the courage
> To let a red sword of virtue
> Plunge into my heart,
> Letting to the weeds of the ground
> My sinful blood,
> What can you offer me?
> A gardened castle?
> A flowery kingdom?
>
> What? A hope?
> Then hence with your red sword of virtue.'
>
> Stephen Crane, *Black Riders* XXX

The eponymous hero of *The Ballad of Cable Hogue* is among the most likeable of Sam Peckinpah's heroes. If Hogue is a morally suspect figure from the point of view of civilization's quasi-religious outlook – Cable, after all, stands for Cain and Abel – his behaviour is consistently legitimate on its own terms. Cable Hogue is nobody's man but his own. A man of the outdoors, he survives through a mixture of guile and industry and even what he eats comes from animals he has killed with his own hands. Peckinpah uses speeded-up motion to underline his hero's freedom from the social constraints that plague the denizens of the world about him. On the one hand, speeded-up motion expresses the vigour of Hogue's life-style, as when Hogue rapidly tidies up his place on Hildy's arrival there. In contrast, when Peckinpah uses it for the film's other two main characters, Joshua, a self-ordained preacher, and Hildy, a prostitute from the nearby town of Deaddog, it is to accentuate states of panic prompted by fear or shame (Hildy disturbed by a stage during her outdoor bath or Joshua disturbed by Claudia's husband as he is about to seduce her).

Left to die in the desert and cursing God for his fate, Cable Hogue stumbles upon a waterhole. Since the hole is near a stage route, he is able to set up a stage depot there and thus earns a living. The area around the waterhole becomes a kind of desert Walden, except that here time seems to stand still. Both Hildy and Joshua make brief stays at the depot, finding in it a refuge from the frontier society that oppresses them. In the early stages of the movie, Peckinpah uses children to suggest a vitality and spontaneity that modern civilization has not yet managed to destroy; and an appearance at the waterhole of children leading an ox-drawn delivery cart provides an image that perfectly encapsulates the innocence and natural vigour which, thanks to Hogue, have come to characterize the place. 'Sun makes 'em real clean', Hogue claims as his excuse for only dousing with water the plates nailed to his outdoor dining-table, and Peckinpah's way of shooting the desert persuades us to believe Hogue's statement. In contrast to his odyssey in the first part of the movie, Hogue's time at the depot is free from storms, the sun never ceasing to shine. According to Max Evans in his book on the making of the film, the whole production was plagued by bad weather. Yet we sense nothing of this except in the overcast dusk skies that Peckinpah uses to provide a romantic backdrop to the love scenes between Cable Hogue and Hildy.

Raoul Walsh's *The Lawless Breed*, Charles Marquis Warren's *Arrowhead*, Richard Fleischer's *These Thousand Hills* – a number of the more intelligent Westerns over the years have sought to subvert the traditional preoccupations of the Western of the twin female protagonists, the demure heroine and the saloon girl. In *The Ballad of Cable Hogue*, however, Peckinpah totally debunks this preoccupation. Claudia, the other key female character to Hildy, has all the primness and poise the Western has traditionally seen as virtues. Yet she is one of the movie's many justifications of Hogue's refusal to adapt to frontier society. Claudia adopts civilized mores, totally unable to comprehend the disparity that exists between these and her more spontaneous self. When Joshua attempts to seduce her under the pretext of offering consolation at the death of her brother, she responds to him because she takes his empty sermonizing as an index of his authority over her. Joshua's attempted seduction of Claudia is actually a parody of her marital life, for her husband treats her with a similar protectiveness and authoritarianism. Hildy, the prostitute, proves superior to Claudia in every way. If Hildy makes love for money, she is at least honest about it. Moreover, she refuses to let Joshua seduce her despite his promise that he will save her soul. When Hildy eventually gives herself to Cable Hogue free of charge, it is for love rather than protection, and she never believes that this gives her any reason to abdicate her autonomy as an individual.

Cable Hogue's love for Hildy is deeply physical; indeed, it is the spectacle of her cleavage that first attracts him to her. But through this Hogue comes to cherish Hildy's spontaneity. For Hogue, Hildy has more honesty and integrity than anyone else in Deaddog, and he does not hesitate to offer her sanctuary in his desert lair when she is hounded out of town. 'Lady, nobody's ever seen you before', he tells her when on the evening of her arrival she emerges from his cabin, wearing a white gown and bathed in the golden shimmer of the dwelling's gaslight. Characteristic of his handling of love relationships, Peckinpah uses water as a symbol for the love of Cable Hogue and Hildy. On the morning after Hogue and Hildy's first night together at the waterhole, the sight of clear water trickling through piping around the waterhole affirms the manner in which the love between them has taken on a fresher, more natural dimension now that Hildy is away from the sordidness of the town. Later, Hogue gives Hildy a bath in the open air. When Hildy insisted Hogue have a bath in town, she was forcing him to comply with standards of social etiquette. But as Hogue baths Hildy, the mood is one of sensuality; it is Hogue's way of expressing his delight in her as a physical being.

'Whatever debts I owe to fate, I'll make fate pay' – a line from one of Richard Gillis' songs in the film aptly sums up the quality of Hogue's self-reliance. During his desert odyssey at the beginning of the movie, he reveals a naive faith in an Old Testament God, yet his attitude to this God is not one of submissiveness. 'You oughta try going dry sometime', he chides Him at first. 'Lord, you call it. I'm done for. Amen' – when Hogue finally calls on this God, it is only to trick him; for as soon as Hogue's foot uncovers a hidden spring, his attitude changes. 'Told you I was gonna live', he defiantly asserts. The damnation *motif* that runs through Peckinpah's work is notably apparent in *The Ballad of Cable Hogue*. Just as he accepts the existence of an Old Testament God, Hogue appears at times to accept that sex is 'base and vile lust', as Joshua puts it. Yet Hogue is so strongly motivated by an inner spontaneity that such a view can never impede his love for Hildy. If he will be damned because of this love, then damned he must be. In this respect he reminds us of Billy's triumphant assumption of a Satan role in *The Deadly Companions*.

In its comic tone, *The Ballad of Cable Hogue* often recalls Mark Twain and the tradition of American humour that surrounds him. In a manner somewhat similar to Twain in *Huckleberry Finn*, Peckinpah uses a semi-literate, down-to-earth hero to expose the hypocrisy of a genteel and formality-ridden culture. When Hogue goes into Deaddog to stake his claim, he runs foul of the bureaucracy there through his manner of doing business: in a memorable scene, he outrages the manager of the stage office when he pours water over the manager's boots to impress on him what he has found.

Much of the movie's comedy derives from the manner pious attitudes are satirized. Unlike in Ford's *Stagecoach* or Boetticher's *The Tall T*, a meeting with a stage in *The Ballad of Cable Hogue* fails to provide the hero with a chance for socially useful action; this is merely used to highlight the fact that the relationship of the hero to civilization is that of a clash of values. As he wanders in the desert at the opening of the movie, Hogue encounters a stagecoach, its passengers a sanctimonious, Bible-quoting husband and wife. In a display of Christian charity, the husband offers Hogue a place in the coach, but his wife is so revolted by Hogue's smell that she refuses to let him enter. The husband then seems to forget Hogue completely and begins to upbraid his wife for undermining his own authority, warning her that 'the wrath of God falls on the children of disobedience'. The conduct of the stage's driver and shotgun, kindred spirits to Hogue, serves further to dissolve the couple's arrogant respectability, the shotgun urinating in earshot of the couple, and the driver tossing a bottle of whiskey to Hogue in flagrant defiance of all notions of temperance.

Sam Peckinpah directing *The Getaway*

Peckinpah directing *The Ballad of Cable Hogue*

Peckinpah directing *Straw Dogs*

John Ford's *My Darling Clementine* –
Wyatt Earp and his id-projection, Doc Holliday

De Mille's *Union Pacific* – a vision of an integrated America

Raoul Walsh's *They Died With Their Boots On* – destiny as violent death

Raoul Walsh's *White Heat* – the manic travesty of the father

Day of the Evil Gun – the prelude to the hero's wounding

Bend of The River – Emerson Cole, a psychopath in search of death

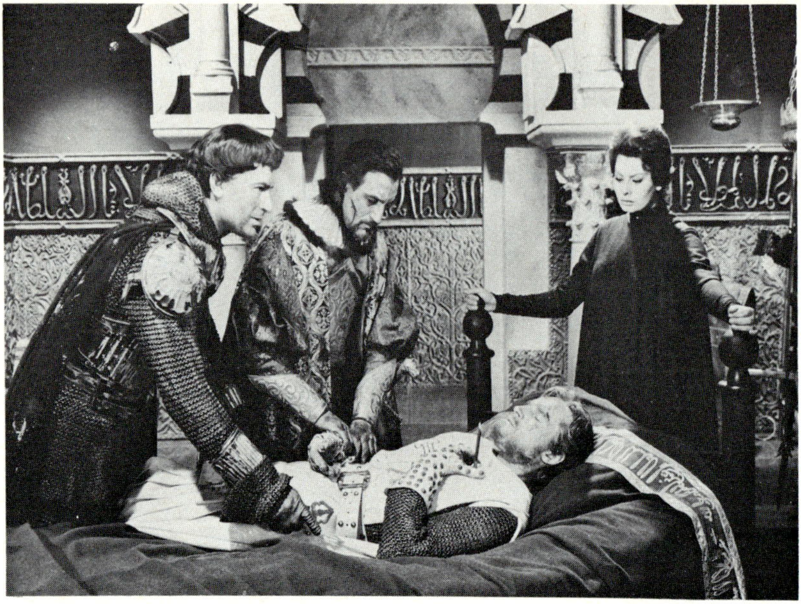

El Cid – death, the wound and separation from woman, the scene prior to El Cid's death

The Wild Bunch – documentary realism

Peckinpah's *Pat Garrett and Billy the Kid* – early morning awakening

The Ballad of Cable Hogue – unfulfilled womanhood

Delmer Daves' *Broken Arrow* – the Indian girl and love in paradise

Peckinpah's *Major Dundee* – Dundee's wounding in a paradisial setting

The devastation of the town of Starbuck at the opening of *The Wild Bunch*

The Deadly Companions
Chill Wills as Turk, the deranged father figure

The church meeting in the saloon – Billy goes to kiss Kit

Kit and Yellowleg – simulated love

Ride the High Country

The oppressiveness of the Knudsen household. Left to right: Joshua Knudsen (R.G.Armstrong), Steve Judd (Joel McCrea), Elsa (Mariette Hartley), Heck (Randy Starr) and Gil Westrum (Randolph Scott)

The Hammond Brothers. Left to right: L.Q.Jones, John Davis Chandler, John Anderson, Warren Oates

The rescue in the Coarse Gold brothel – Steve Judd in defence of the maternal principle

Before the final gunfight

Major Dundee

The capture of Tyreen (Richard Harris) by Dundee (Charlton Heston) – a scene cut by the producer

Dundee's interview with Samuel Potts (James Coburn), watched by Ryan (Michael Anderson Jnr)

The digging of the mass grave

The death of Tyreen – Dundee's id-projection claims its rights

The death of Tyreen

The Wild Bunch

The Wild Bunch. Left to right: Tector Gorch (Ben Johnson), Lyle Gorch (Warren Oates), Pike Bishop (William Holden), Dutch (Ernest Borgnine)

Mapache (Emilio Fernandez) slits the throat of Angel (Jaime Sanchez)

Dutch struggles towards Pike Bishop to die

Pike Bishop's memory of being slapped by the only woman he ever loved – before being gunned down by her husband

The Ballad of Cable Hogue

Taggart (L.Q.Jones) and Bowen (Strother Martin) threatened by Hogue's snakes

Cable Hogue (Jason Robards Jnr) sees through the show of humility put on by Joshua (David Warner)

Hogue and Hildy (Stella Stevens)

Straw Dogs

David Sumner (Dustin Hoffman) and Amy (Susan George) – absence of communication

Confrontation before the siege. Left to right: Scutt (Ken Hutchinson), David Sumner (Dustin Hoffman), Cawsey (Jim Norton), Venner (Del Henney)

Charlie Venner about to kill Norman Scutt

Junior Bonner

The brawl in the Palace Bar

Junior (Steve McQueen) and Charmagne (Barbara Leigh)

Ace (Robert Preston) and Elvira Bonner (Ida Lupino)

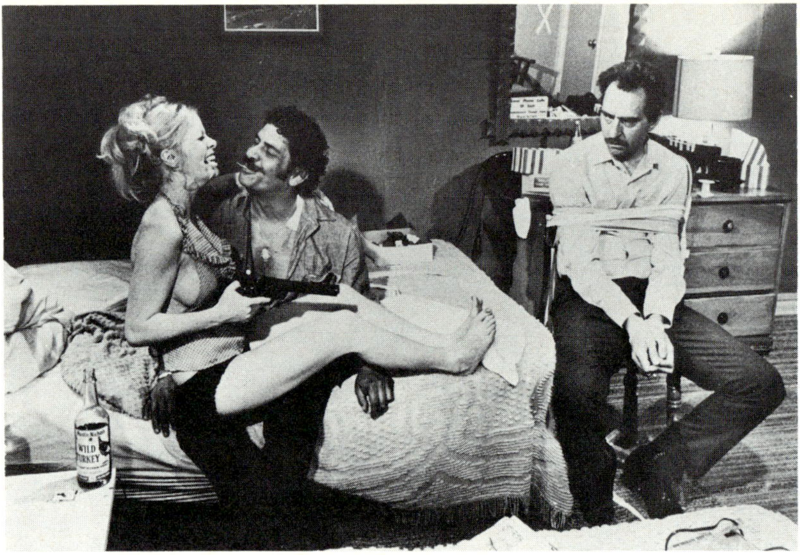

The Getaway

Rudy (Al Lettieri) with Fran (Sally Struthers) and Harold (Jack Dobson) – echoes of the primal scene

From the climactic shoot-out in the El Paso hotel – Doc McCoy (Steve McQueen) and Carol (Ali McGraw)

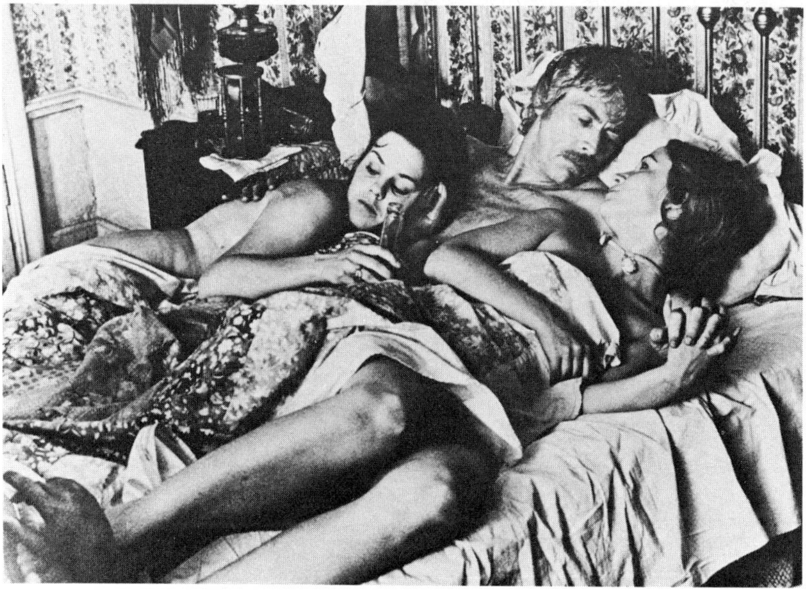

Pat Garrett and Billy the Kid

Garrett (James Coburn) proves his virility with prostitutes

Billy (Kris Kristofferson) is menaced by Ollinger (R.G.Armstrong)

Garrett attacks Poe (John Beck) after the killing of Billy

Bring me the Head of Alfredo Garcia
The girl (Janine Maldonado) is tortured

Elita (Isela Vega) is attacked by Paco (Kris Kristofferson)

Bennie (Warren Oates) wakes in the grave to find Elita dead

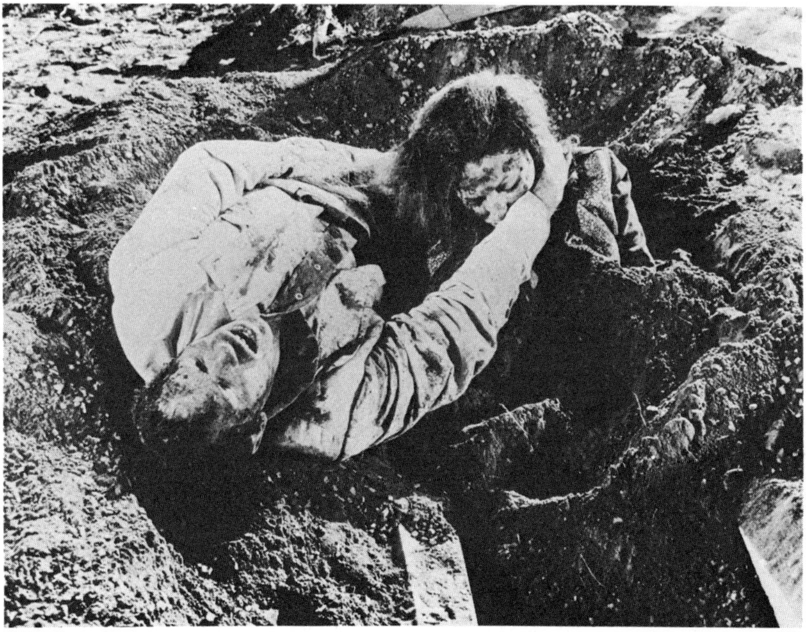

Bennie takes on El Jefe's men

Bennie's shoot out with El Jefe's men

The Killer Elite

Locken (James Caan) first meets Miller, the 'psycho' (Bo Hopkins)

Hansen (Robert Duvall) in ambush

Weyburn (Gig Young) and Collis (Arthur Hill) in conference

Locken in the taxi of Mac (Burt Young)

Locken fights with his walking stick in the climactic battle

Cross of Iron

Steiner (James Coburn) discovers the Russian boy (Slavco Stimac) on the battle-field

The child hands Steiner the mouth-organ

Captain Stransky (Maximilian Schell)

Eva (Senta Berger)

The German platoon and the captured Russian women's unit

Steiner seeking revenge

The death of Schnurrbart

Hogue also exposes the fraudulence of the so-called Christian values 'Preacher' Joshua claims to represent. When, on his first visit to the waterhole, Joshua puts on a display of Christian kindness in the hope of obtaining a free drink, Hogue is characteristically terse in his treatment of him: 'Pay up, you pious bastard.' Despite all of the sermonizing, Joshua's visit is only important to Hogue in that it has a practical value: through Joshua, Hogue learns that he must stake a claim in town and is provided with a horse that he can commandeer for this purpose. Riding away on Joshua's horse, Hogue thanks the preacher for having shown him 'the way to salvation'.

The fundamental distinction between Hogue and Joshua is an existentialist one. This is made clear in a comic discourse they have about women. Joshua commences to praise women as manifestations of God's bounty, commenting on how the Lord has had the foresight to locate a women's breasts in just the right place. But Hogue refuses to see anything special in this: 'Where the hell else would he put them? On her backside?' When Joshua proceeds to extol God for creating women's legs, Hogue refuses to see these in anything but concrete terms: 'Some go all the way up to the lady's ass; some stop somewhat below.' To Joshua, religious faith is the belief that essence precedes existence; he wants reasons and excuses for the way life is. On the other hand, Hogue may have a vague belief in a divine being but he is incapable of seeing him as a master craftsman behind the whole creation. Hogue believes foremost in existence, in the concrete and real world; it is enough for him that life simply *is* of its own accord.

The Ballad of Cable Hogue is Peckinpah's corrective to the Bible's book of Genesis. It is not woman nor the serpent that can disrupt the harmony of Hogue's 'cactus Eden', as Joshua calls it, but the values of which Joshua is himself a harbinger. Just as woman in the form of Hildy brings joy to Hogue's waterhole, so the serpent exists there as a proud and dignified creature rather than as an incarnation of evil. Hogue captures rattle-snakes and keeps them as pets; and these function in the movie as symbols for his virility. When Hogue's snakes escape from a bag Joshua is carrying, Joshua flees in terror while Hogue calmly retrieves the animals, handling them with ease. At the end of the movie, Hogue uses his snakes to scare Taggart and Bowen, the two rogues who left him to die in the desert and who now wish to violate his desert Eden.

By relegating man to a secondary place in the scheme of things, Joshua has also lost faith in himself; beneath his boasts about his prowess with women lies a desperate insecurity. In the scene where Hildy leaves the waterhole, Joshua reveals a strange empathy with Hogue. 'Every once in a while one of them cuts straight into you', he confides in a dejected Hogue on the subject of women. 'When you die, you forget her.' Here, Joshua gives himself away: it seems he really cared for a woman in the past but now he can only feel regret at the manner in which the society about him has destroyed his capacity to love. Yet although he feels a respect for Hogue's capacity to love, Joshua is driven by envy to try and assume the role of Hogue's repressive conscience. All that Joshua succeeds in doing is sealing his own isolation. This is made particularly evident in the scene where Joshua accompanies Hogue in going to pay court to Hildy in Deaddog's brothel. Joshua is left lingering at the door of Hildy's room after Hogue has entered; he listens to the sexy sounds that come from within the room, but it is as if some magic charm prevents him from entering to disturb the intimacy of Hogue and Hildy. This is followed by the scene where Joshua picks up Claudia and they are disturbed by Claudia's authoritarian husband, Joshua's love-making frustrated in a manner Joshua would have liked to frustrate that of Hogue. Expressive of the workings of Joshua's own repressive conscience, this scene provides a comic equivalent of the woundings of Major Dundee and Pike Bishop.

The movie's opening scene of its hero's abandonment in the desert establishes a conflict between Hogue's natural instinct to survive, with its fundamental reverence for life, and a rapacity whose aims are the subjugation of life and wanton destructiveness. When Hogue is about to kill a lizard for food, Taggart blasts it to pieces with his shotgun, similarities with the blasting of a lizard in *The Treasure of the Sierra Madre* only deepening the ecological resonances of Taggart's callousness. When Taggart insists to Bowen, his stooge, that they abandon Hogue, he seems to be doing it more out of malice than to conserve water supplies. Like Joshua, Taggart envies Hogue; his own obsessive need to prove himself a man seems to spring from his deformed hand. In the first shot of the movie Hogue's shadow falls across the lizard he intends to catch and eat; this symbolism is later re-echoed in the first meeting between Joshua and Hogue when Joshua's shadow falls across Hogue, establishing a link between Hogue and the cornered animal of the opening. This shot emphasizes that although Hogue cannot be corrupted by the values of men like Joshua and Taggart, his own lifestyle is nevertheless menaced by these values.

Throughout the movie, heroic notions are played out against the social reality of a changing West. The first part of the movie has obvious parallels with the beginning of Howard Hawks' *Red River*: Peckinpah's hero survives the hazards of the desert, discovers a waterhole and is forced to draw on a man who objects to being his first paying customer; Hawks' hero, Tom Dunson, survives the rigours of a wagon trek, comes upon a piece of fertile land and kills a Mexican who contests his claim. Yet whereas Dunson went on to build a cattle empire, Hogue merely establishes a stage depot. Indeed, Hogue never attains full heroic stature. This is even denied him by the film's visuals. Hogue is seldom seen on horseback, the traditional dominant pose of the Western hero, and at times he seems an extremely vulnerable figure as he ambles about his desert lair.

Although Hogue discovers the waterhole and defends it against intruders, the place is only properly his after he has been to town to file a claim – filing a claim, of course, was something Tom Dunson never felt compelled to do. Peckinpah's treatment of the law is characteristically ironic: the law in this case seems to exist to sanction acts of rapacity rather than to prevent them. Hogue's visit to Deaddog to file his claim, if it begins comically, takes on a tragic tone as Hogue can find no one to provide him with financial backing to set up a stage depot. '*I'm* worth something, ain't I?' Hogue pleads with a bank president, who asks after collateral; and it is only then that the president relents and gives him some money.

Hogue is not without complicity in his final downfall. As with Potts in *Major Dundee*, the only means of self expression Hogue can find lies in furthering the march of a civilization that can have no place for him. The Bible-quoting husband and wife; the travellers who nosily peer from a coach to disturb Hildy's bath; the women who, with comically contorted gait, scurry to the depot's john (a sad contrast with the stage shotgun's brazen urination in the desert) – these are the people the stage is bringing West to swell the townships, people whose way of life is diametrically opposed to Hogue's; and yet through the establishment of his depot Hogue is encouraging their migration. The film contains a split-screen sequence of Hogue feverishly busy in different kinds of activity building the depot and a montage sequence of different shots of the stage passing superimposed over a shot of Hogue bellowing his name; but within the narrative framework these come as ways of paying tribute to Hogue's power and vitality, rather than creating a sense of anything permanent and solid being achieved. The scene where Hogue first raises the American flag above the depot invites a complex response. In one respect, it encourages admiration for what Hogue's tenacity has achieved. Yet, if viewed in the light of Hogue's deal with the stage line, it becomes a demonstration of how capitalism under the guise of nationalism annexes itself to individuals' acts of rapacity.

With the coming of the car, social change reaches a point where it denies Hogue a sphere of action altogether and makes it impossible for him to exercise control over his fate any longer. When Taggart and Bowen reappear to rob Hogue of his money, Hogue is forced to kill Taggart. Yet, soon after the showdown is over, a car passes the depot and its occupants laugh coldly and heartlessly at the distraught Bowen, illustrating that modern society can be capable of a cruelty even beyond Taggart's.

Social change also finally forces the love of Hogue and Hildy to a dead end. Hogue's preoccupation with defining himself through power after his abandonment by Taggart and Bowen continually proves an obstacle to his relationship with Hildy. On his first visit to Hildy's room, Hogue is too worried about having left Joshua on his claim to bother to make love to Hildy and she retaliates by insisting that he pay her money for his visit. Later, at the waterhole, Hildy's idyll with Hogue is brought to an end when in an angry mood over Joshua not paying board Hogue compliments Hildy on not charging him for sex. Tormented by the memory she is a prostitute, Hildy leaves the waterhole and heads for San Francisco. After he kills Taggart, Hogue acknowledges the futility of his revenge by giving his waterhole to Bowen; through this gesture, Hogue reveals that he is still sufficiently uncorrupted by social values to be able to choose love to power. Unfortunately Hildy has by this time unwittingly become a force that can destroy Hogue. 'In town I'd be nothing and I don't want to be nothing', Hogue tells Hildy, early in their affair. But Hildy still seeks to persuade Hogue to leave his waterhole; and after she has made it rich in San Francisco, she returns to take Hogue away with her. When Hildy asks Hogue if he is ready to leave, he replies in a fatalistic tone: 'Hell, I've already left.' Then, as Hildy and Hogue kiss, Peckinpah cuts to the heat gauge of Hildy's car so that this appears to be registering the intensity of their experience, a characteristic affirmation of Peckinpah that the dynamism of human beings is more powerful than that of machines. Yet Hildy's car kills Hogue before he can leave the waterhole. Innocent of the car's workings, Hogue accidentally knocks off its brake and falls under it himself after pushing Bowen out of its path. As so often in Peckinpah's movies, the hero's death, if unexpected, provides the only resolution to the drama. Death at least provides Hogue with a means of escaping a civilization that would only destroy him as a person.

Before he dies, Hogue reaffirms the invincibility of his love for Hildy. Hildy tells him about how the rich old man she married in San Francisco died from a stroke in bed, and whereas so many of Peckinpah's heroes would have beaten or even killed the woman they loved for openly admitting to sex with someone else, Hogue bursts merrily into laughter, a laughter that is shared by the stage's shotgun, its driver and Hildy herself. Nothing can destroy Hogue's belief in the genuineness of Hildy's affection for him.

When, after the accident, Joshua arrives – on a motorcycle! – Hogue explains to him humorously: 'Just dying; last reckoning.' But Joshua goes into a pompous funeral oration, distorting and rendering meaningless everything that Hogue has stood for. Suddenly Peckinpah cuts to the end of the funeral: it is night and the mourners leave; the stage-office manager looks at his watch angry that he has wasted so much time at the funeral. Peckinpah has never been one for funerals in his movies – the mass burial in *Major Dundee* is a kind of parody of a Fordian military funeral – and most likely he could not be bothered to dwell on the community's ritual leave-taking of Cable Hogue because he thought this would be too great an insult to his hero. For all its warmth and lyricism, *The Ballad of Cable Hogue* remains as much an open wound as any of Sam Peckinpah's other movies.

CHAPTER SIX: STRAW DOGS

Straw Dogs has a bizarre pedigree. It is credited with being based on a novel called *The Siege of Trencher's Farm* by Gordon Williams, and from the novel it takes its basic plot situation – that of a run-in between an American academic and the locals of a remote English village where he is spending a sabbatical. At the same time, an uncredited but significant influence appears to have been Jean-Paul Sartre's *The Flies*. Peckinpah's academic and his English wife, David and Amy Sumner, who seek to take a stand against the corruptness of the village, recall in many ways Sartre's brother and sister, Orestes and Electra, battling against the tyranny of Argos. The movie's title is from yet another source – the *Tao-Te-Ching* by Lao-Tzu, a Chinese mystic. Straw dogs instead of real dogs were used at Chinese religious ceremonies as sacrificial objects. The title thus sums up the relationship between individual and society that Peckinpah seeks to present in his movie.

If *Straw Dogs* fails in a number of ways, it remains of interest in that it is Peckinpah's first attempt to examine the preoccupations of the Western in a non-generic context. If it succeeds in nothing else, it manages to clarify the Gothic nature of these preoccupations.

Straw Dogs' English village is more like a Western township than a Cornish village. It is an oppressive place: its priest, Reverend Hood, and its 'lawman', Major Scott, are seen to contribute to the general uneasiness in the manner they carry out their appointed roles as custodians of order. The main concern of both men is to maintain what is conventionally regarded as an acceptable standard of behaviour among the villagers, all of which never results in anything more than a grotesque parody of conventional etiquette. Despite aggressive displays of individuality, the villagers for the most part never rebel against the authority of priest and 'lawman' with anything but a pathetic rudeness – Tom Hedden gives a mocking salute and sticks out his tongue when the Major makes him drink up his pint at closing-time, while at a church social Charlie Venner and his cronies also treat Sumner with a reverence similar to that with which they treat the priest and the Major, often calling him 'sir' and feigning obsequiousness. Up until the final showdown, their acts of meanness towards Sumner are always done behind his back.

Fundamentally, the community derives what cohesiveness it has from the incest taboo. Tom Hedden is in many ways the true head of the community. Zealously overprotective of his young daughter, Hedden recalls Joshua Knudsen in *Ride the High Country.* Obsessed with displaying their virility and plagued with anxieties about women, the young men of the village rally around the patriarchal figure of Hedden. It is fitting that the only sex we see in the movie should be the rape of Amy Sumner by Charlie Venner and his friend, Norman Scutt. Rape to the rapist is usually tantamount to incest, the forbidden and forbidding woman a symbol for the mother, so, in their rape of Amy, Venner and Scutt can be seen to be acting out the contradictions that lie at the heart of the community. When Venner rapes Amy for whom he feels a strange affection and then lets Scutt take her from him, Venner's total aquiescence to Scutt – he even holds Amy down for him – cannot be explained away totally by the fact that Scutt is brandishing a shotgun; it seems that, in his deference to Scutt, Venner compulsively feels himself to be acknowledging the father's prior claim to the mother. Scutt, on the other hand, rapes Amy after she has been raped by someone else, thus by implication seeking to humiliate the mother for being the father's property. Yet Venner and Scutt can shirk any shame for their actions: since Amy is a local girl who has married a foreigner, they are able to see themselves as reclaiming one of the daughters of the community from an alien who has made an unnatural claim on her.

It is in defence of the incest taboo that the community is finally driven to violence. When Tom Hedden, Venner, Scutt, the village ratcatcher and another man set out to have revenge on Henry Niles, the village idiot, for assaulting Janet Hedden, they do not even have proof that anything has happened; it is enough that they suspect the girl may have been 'threatened'. With the five men driven on by an irrational fury all hell breaks loose.

Henry Niles, the only likeable character in the village, is certainly not the raving madman the villagers make him out to be. When he kills Janet Hedden, it is quite by accident: she herself lures him out into the fog to try to seduce him, and the actual killing is caused by Tom Hedden's outraged voice scaring him so that he unwittingly stifles the girl in a protective embrace. Unable to dissimilate from others or from himself, Niles is genuinely terrified and confused after killing the girl; and when Venner and Scutt subsequently assert that he is a pervert, they are merely making their own duplicity all the more clear. Of all the characters in Straw Dogs, Niles is the one who acts most fully out of that inner spontaneity that Peckinpah values so highly.

In his scene with Janet Hedden prior to her death, Niles emerges as a truly heroic character. As the two of them embrace, Peckinpah cuts to the church social where the priest leads a group of candle-bearing children in a prayer against sin; this bizarre and non-naturalistic scene provides a visual representation of the workings of the community's conscience. Yet unwittingly defying the priest's tirade, Niles goes ahead and kisses the girl. Seen in terms of the ensuing violence, Niles' kiss comes as the first spark ignited by Eros to explode the repressive status quo of the village.

The marriage of David and Amy Sumner is an insubstantial thing. Their sex life appears to be one long arousal without an orgasm: they indulge in a nervy petting game in their car while Sumner is actually driving it, and when he gets into bed with his wife, he delays embracing her until after he has removed his watch and wound up the alarm clock. More seriously, however, their relationship appears to be infected by the incest taboo that plagues the village. Their petting is watched by Janet Hedden and her brother, whose gleeful cuddling carries suggestions of an incest fantasy. Then, when Sumner is about to have sexual intercourse with his wife, Peckinpah cuts to the village pub where Scutt is waving Amy's stolen knickers at Venner as if to show his prior claim to her, the scene coming as a subliminal representation of Sumner's own feelings of exclusion from his wife, particularly since in the next scene Sumner and wife are seated apart in the study, bickering with one another.

'Every chair is my daddy's chair', Amy boasts to Sumner. The remark is revealing because it shows she wants her husband to measure up to her father and indicates that she can only relate to men as authority figures. Desire for a father figure and the sexual inadequacy of her husband drive Amy towards Charlie Venner. In the first scene of the movie, Venner dotes on Amy, stroking her hair as if she is a child; and Amy proves not unresponsive to his promise to take care of her. When Venner turns up at the house while Sumner is out shooting, Amy lets him in. He refuses to leave, so she slaps him; and when he slaps her back, she becomes totally passive. She lies down whimpering as Venner removes her clothes. 'I don't want to rape you but I will', he threatens as she begins to object. So she stays quiet and he rapes her anyway. She looks at the hearth-fire guarded by grating as if searching for some image of comfort, and then she pulls Venner down to her and kisses him affectionately, trying to convince herself that he is her lover. When Sumner returns, she tells him nothing about the rape, and as he touches her in bed, her mind goes back to the rape and flashbacks to this scene are so intercut by Peckinpah that Sumner himself appears to be her violator. Later, during the siege at the house, it is Venner to whom Amy turns for protection rather than her husband.

Though David Sumner is writing a thesis on a lofty mathematical theme, he is still a man at the mercy of more primitive urges. The sight of blood totally mesmerizes him – in the village pub he dotes upon the bleeding hand that the bartender has cut, and later he is fascinated by the cut lip of Niles caused by a slap from his brother. Sumner's behaviour becomes increasingly erratic as he is drawn into the butch world of the village males. *Straw Dogs* is full of sub-Sartrian talk about commitment and it frequently seems that Peckinpah wants us to take as purer than they are his hero's motives for gradually opposing himself to the villagers. But they remain ambiguous: when Sumner is sarcastic to the village priest, there may be truth in his words, but his aggressiveness clearly seems inspired by his fascination with Venner and his crew. The violence in the villagers is also symbolically linked with Sumner's potentiality for violence – Amy's cat, which Sumner resents, is killed by the villagers, and Sumner finally kills Venner with the steel trap in which previously Scutt has jestingly attempted to ensnare Venner. Moreover, as it is for the village males so the lure of violence for Sumner is bound up with anxieties about women. Sumner's surrender to the lure of violence appears as the consequence of his exclusion from his wife. As Venner and Scutt prepare to rape his wife, Sumner is out shooting, tricked into doing so by them. When Amy embraces Venner in acknowledgement that she has been sexually fulfilled at last, Sumner is shown shooting a bird and then retrieving it from a bush, contemplating its blood on his hand. The effect of this cutting is to suggest that Sumner, unable to be a man in the bedroom with his wife, is asserting a claim to manhood through violence.

In *Straw Dogs* Peckinpah masterfully depicts a society torn apart by violence. He makes his audience aware of the incongruous juxtaposition of modern and primitive values and attitudes: in a 'cosy' domestic scene, Sumner pelts his wife's cat with grapefruit and tomatoes as classical music blurts from a transistor radio; while on a more dramatic level, an aria from *Rigoletto* is heard at the church social as the village males begin their bloodthirsty hunt for Niles. Everything seems to have two sides: ostensibly harmless and yet violent. On the sunny Sunday morning with which the film opens, a church bell is tolling. This tolling, merging out of the discordant notes of Jerry Fielding's score and accompanying the gradually focussing image of a boy sitting on a tombstone, gives the impression of order barely imposed on chaos. When next the bell is heard tolling, it is night and it heralds danger and destruction: Janet Hedden is believed missing and the village males round on Sumner's cottage where they know Niles to be hiding. At the church social, flashback memory images of the rape of Sumner's wife are sandwiched between shots of the priest so as to make him appear a rapist, libidinous forces seeming to heave beneath the surface of the community. The cutting during the siege is so abrupt that at moments all sense of time and space are lost – a tilted shot of Niles in panic is followed by a huge close-up of a rat, Amy in panic inside the cottage is followed by the ratcatcher cavorting about on a tricycle outside.

In the climax of *Straw Dogs*, Peckinpah reiterates with greater explicitness an idea that was implicit in the opening of *The Wild Bunch* – namely, that a society unable to accommodate basic drives deserves to be torn to shreds. Here, Peckinpah chronicles how a patriarchal society destroys itself by its very incestuousness. Tom Hedden guns down the Major, whom he has always secretly resented. Venner kills Scutt when Scutt again tries to assert a claim to Amy.

Yet the climax of *Straw Dogs* is severely marred by the manner Peckinpah seeks to accord a lofty moral righteousness to his hero's actions. Whereas most of Peckinpah's heroes consign themselves to solitude and yet find themselves forced to acknowledge a dependence on others, David Sumner remains a resolute solipsist.

What was happening to Sam Peckinpah when he made *Straw Dogs?* Was he having a crisis in his personal life? As it progresses, *Straw Dogs* becomes increasingly the product of a mind in a state of utter desperation. Of course, there is basically nothing wrong with a great director making a movie when he feels unduly tormented. Yet what makes the pessimism of *Straw Dogs* so distressing is that it involves such a regression in Peckinpah's humanism.

'Smell a rat, see a rat, kill a rat. Life is rats' – the village ratcatcher's advice to Sumner is given credibility by the general nastiness of almost everyone in the movie. Although co-scriptwriter Goodman might be responsible for this black view of human nature – in the doting cruelty of its characters, *Straw Dogs* recalls Terence Fisher's Goodman-scripted *The Stranglers of Bombay* – it is difficult not to see also in this attitude the vilificatory puritan, the Joshua Knudsen, in Peckinpah surfacing unchecked. When Sumner pulls his wife's hair to prevent her from opening the door to Venner, or slaps Niles to make him quiet, there is a wild jubilation to his behaviour, as if he has only just learned this is the way to treat people. It is one thing for Peckinpah – as he does in most of his movies – to celebrate primitive energy as evidence of the human personality's essential inability to be fully coerced by any status quo; in *Straw Dogs* he tries to claim that this energy is moral in itself, and, like Jack London before him, he merely ends up endorsing brute force.

Peckinpah seemed to have in mind for the end of *Straw Dogs* a similar moral equation to the one which Sartre achieved in *The Flies*. He tries to present Sumner as a kindred spirit to Sartre's Orestes, having him recurrently profess his resolve to take a stand. Yet although he has implied his hero's sexual impotence earlier in the movie, Peckinpah refuses to take this into consideration at all during the climax; in fact, one wonders just how consciously he has been handling this theme. In the Wild Bunch's last stand, irrational motivation (an impulse to rebel against loneliness and impotence) managed to complement rational motivation (a desire to affirm solidarity), but Sumner's implied sexual impotence makes his supposedly heroic stand seem something of a sham. Indeed, it seems at times as if Peckinpah is not just asserting that violence attests to the continuing force of Eros denied a sexual outlet, but that he actually believes that virility displayed through violence is preferable to sexual virility. This is born out by Peckinpah's praise after completing the movie for the ideas of Robert Ardrey, who makes crude claims about how men are motivated by predatory principles similar to animals. Ardrey's *The Territorial Imperative*, for instance, claims that the defence of territory is a natural and spontaneous thing; and one can imagine Peckinpah involving himself with such ideas so as to blind himself to the sexual frustration underlying Sumner's motivation.

When, after the siege, Sumner leaves with Henry Niles to drive off into the night, he is not much better off than Major Dundee left holding the American flag. When he defended Niles, the man who dared the forbidden kiss, Sumner was symbolically defending a surrogate for his phallic self and not really taking responsibility for that self. Yet, by giving Sumner 'significant' lines about not knowing his way home, Peckinpah finally seems to want us to believe that Sumner has made a fully-fledged acceptance of an Oedipal destiny. To do this, however, Sumner would need to view his relationship with his wife from a rational perspective.

It is difficult to condemn Amy Sumner as much as Peckinpah insists we ought. Whereas Electra in *The Flies* decides to accept a corrupt status quo, Amy is bullied into doing so. Peckinpah's moral down-grading of Amy seems most likely prompted by his refusal to see his hero's shortcomings. As with vilificatory puritanism, so with misogyny, perhaps: if through Angel's slaying of Teresa in *The Wild Bunch* Peckinpah was able to expose a peculiarly American misogyny and a perverse side of the Western, he appears to fall prey completely to this misogyny himself in his treatment of Amy in *Straw Dogs*.

Yet we must expect a drive towards the disproportionate in the work of a man who so clearly creates art from the storm centre of his emotions. *Straw Dogs* is the only movie where Peckinpah goes completely overboard, and it is not entirely perverse: if at times it comes close to the schoolboy heroics of a *High Noon* or a *Rio Bravo*, it nevertheless reveals a certain American attitude to toughness as the legacy of patriarchal oppression. Setting out to endorse butch values, it unwittingly shows that these have their roots in sexual impotence. Sumner's final leave-taking of his wife after having won the big fight may echo the Western convention of the hero's final ride into the distance, yet it reveals this convention to be the product of an appalling cultural dislocation.

CHAPTER SEVEN: JUNIOR BONNER

Junior Bonner is Peckinpah's first movie set in the present-day West. It tells of a homecoming. After a year away playing the rodeo circuits, Junior Bonner returns to his home town of Prescott, Arizona. The way of life that bred Junior is in its dying throes: the money men are carving up the prairie to sell it and putting its animals in cages. The machine is nightmarishly in control: the crew who demolish the shack of Ace Bonner, Junior's father, are strange anonymous figures, their faces concealed by protective masks (a 'facelessness' re-echoed in the subsequent rodeo scenes, with so many characters wearing sunglasses). The patriarchal authority of Peckinpah's previous Westerns has now given way to an anonymous authority. The money market, so-called good sense, moderation, 'bourgeois' respectability – these are the ridiculous forces that now control people's lives.

As the movie opens a dejected Junior is returning from a failed attempt to ride a black bull called Sunshine. Peckinpah uses a split-screen technique to present monochrome flashbacks to Junior riding the bull, an elated experience to which Junior harks back (the subliminal nature of these flashbacks is stressed by the fact that they are non-sequential, Junior seen first riding the bull, then mounting it). A similar juxtaposition introduces Ace Bonner: a flashback to Ace riding a mount in his days of glory as a rodeo star precedes the old man's appearance in the sterilized confines of a hospital ward where he is recovering from an accident he brought upon himself through drunken driving.

Zoom shots, cut before they have time to linger on a point of interest, provide an appropriate means of describing the dislocations of Junior's homecoming, Peckinpah zooming in on an object Junior finds unsettling and usually juxtaposing this with a zoom to his hero's incredulous face. Peckinpah also produces jarring effects by intercutting long-shots with close-shots. The demolition of Ace's shack seems like the encroachment of impersonal forces, since the spectacle of a bulldozer in the act of demolition is intercut with a photograph inside the shack of Ace in his rodeo past. The same technique also works to create the impression of anarchic elements writhing beneath the impact of a paralysing social fabric. The brief close-ups of Ace's barking dog or the strange moment when a clown on a motorcycle drives forward staring at the camera – these and other appropriately jarring images continually punctuate panoramic viewpoints of rodeo proceedings.

The West of *Junior Bonner* is in dire paralysis. Peckinpah underlines what has become of the anarchic spirit of the Wild Bunch when, during Prescott's rodeo parade, an inane-looking man in a black suit rides past on a nag which has 'the Wild Bunch' lettered on its saddlecloth. One of the wildest things in *Junior Bonner* is Ace's mangy but belligerent hound, who will 'either shake your hand or bite it off'. Another embodiment of wildness is Sunshine, the black bull Junior is out to ride; its freedom cruelly circumscribed, this magnificent animal lives forever enclosed by fences.

The parade that begins Prescott's rodeo is an uninspiring sight: mountain men, cavalry, and Indians thick with war-paint dutifully take their places among advertising floats, schoolchildren, and police and army displays; the sight of a baby's naked backside protruding from amid a crowd only serves to highlight the absence of unforced naturalness in the proceedings themselves. Old-time wildness can never really re-assert itself. When the horses on which Junior is riding with his father break into a gallop, the havoc caused is far from that wrought by the Wild Bunch among the Temperance marchers; Junior and Ace career through suburbs until a collision with a washing-line unhorses them and they are given a ticking-off by an irate housewife. Peckinpah uses slow motion for the collision with the washing-line, yet the effect created is not one of energy exploding but of physical clumsiness. The din of the rodeo crowds also seems to depersonalize the visuals. Laughter, its function so affirmative in *The Wild Bunch* and *The Ballad of Cable Hogue*, exists largely in a debased form in *Junior Bonner*. The rodeo crowds are unamused by the antics of Junior and Ace during the procession; from Junior and Ace in the suburbs, Peckinpah keeps cutting back to the parade where the crowd's laughter is drawn by the programmed anarchy of the rodeo clowns.

The rodeo scenes are largely unheroic. For the first half of the rodeo a succession of shots – some in slow motion – of riders vainly trying to stay on their beasts is intercut with close-ups of a hooter buzzing; these buzzes signify the passage of the eight seconds for which the riders are required to stay mounted. The cutting for this sequence is so fast that the sensations of the riders are never fully conveyed; when one rider does have a nasty fall, there is simply an abrupt cut to him being hurriedly bundled into an ambulance. Over the whole proceedings a compere's voice maintains a god-like aloofness through loudspeakers; having introduced one contestant, the voice hurriedly moves on to the next.

Only at interval-time in the Palace Bar does the rodeo world seem briefly to regain its former vitality. As a fight begins over Junior making a pass at another man's girl and disorder spreads throughout the bar, Peckinpah rapidly cuts between different characters until the screen appears to bustle with activity. People who do not join in the brawl respond to it by falling about laughing or abandoning themselves to necking. Observing the scene, Del, the old bartender who has a picture of Ace above his bar, lets out a long hearty laugh – the most memorable instance of genuine laughter in the movie. The frolic is brought to a close by the group's rendering of 'The Star-spangled Banner', and a stark contrast to the forced patriotism of the rodeo's official opening is made by the lines of smiling faces that greet this tune. Appropriately, the saloon brawl serves both as the occasion for the rekindling of love between Ace and his wife, Elvira, and as a prelude to Junior's second attempt at riding Sunshine. This time Junior succeeds in riding the bull, and the hooter's buzzing of the eight seconds is for once drowned by the roar of the crowd – another instance in Peckinpah of sheer physical dynamism triumphing over machine.

Junior Bonner's dilemma is succinctly established at the beginning of the movie by the split-screen flashbacks to his riding Sunshine. After his first attempt to ride Sunshine, Junior goes to see the black bull in its corral, and when it chases and almost injures him, this only increases Junior's fascination with the animal. Subliminal flashbacks to Junior riding the bull recur throughout the film, and, like Sumner's sightings of blood in *Straw Dogs*, these seem in the movie's overall context like effusions of living matter onto the dead surface of society. Peckinpah also intercuts flashbacks of Junior's first attempt to ride Sunshine with Junior's final successful attempt, creating the impression of individual and external reality briefly reconciled, of a 'super-reality' attained.

Much of the time, Junior behaves like a sleep-walker, so absorbed is he in his inner world of primitive violence. In his relationship with Charmagne, the girl he picks up in the Palace Bar, Junior is merely externalizing his obsession with the black bull. By prefiguring the meeting of Junior and Charmagne in the bar with the juxtaposition of zoom shots on each of them, Peckinpah emphasizes that it is a physical pull that draws Junior to Charmagne. With her raven hair, supple skin and natural vitality, Charmagne reminds Junior of the black bull; she is even jokingly compared to Sunshine by Red Terwilliger, a fellow rodeo star.

Junior values his independence highly. When Charmagne tells him she has a boring job working in a bank, Junior replies that her job would only be interesting if she owned the bank; he just cannot make sense of a world populated almost exclusively by employees of big corporations. Junior has little money but he refuses to take jobs that could make him rich; he is offered employment both by Curly, his brother, and Buck Roan, a big-time rodeo impresario. When Curly suggests to Junior that he ought to try and earn a million dollars like himself, Junior simply replies: 'I got to go down my own road.' For him the lifetime of 'bourgeois' security that a million dollars can buy is worth less than those occasional eight seconds of communion with primitive violence.

Unlike many of Peckinpah's other heroes, there is little psychological depth to the character of Junior Bonner. This is why the movie, for all its stylish set pieces, is minor Peckinpah. All the issues he could not confront in *Straw Dogs* Peckinpah brushes aside totally in *Junior Bonner*, choosing to romanticize the inveterate professionalism of the Steve McQueen *persona*. If Junior prefers the primitive violence of bull-riding to women and has a thing about being 'lonesome', Peckinpah never really sees this as narcissistic; and if there is a virago-like predatoriness to Charmagne when she first sights Junior, this provides only a slight and momentary threat to the hero's masculinity. Most of the time, Peckinpah romanticizes Junior's behaviour as springing from a noble attachment to the frontier and its values. Junior's reverence for the old-time wildness is underlined by his taking custody of Ace's hound after this has been ejected from the family home by Curly.

'All we got left is today', Ace tells his estranged wife, seeking to convince her he is about to head for Australia and gold so that she will consent to make love to him. These words sum up Ace; philandering, drinking and hatching wild schemes, he lives for the moment. Though something of a physical wreck, he derives a certain dignity from his inability to bow down to society's rules. Few people in the rodeo crowds remember who he is, yet he borrows Junior's horse and takes his place right at the head of the rodeo procession, while Curly, his other son, takes an allotted place in the commercial section.

Both Junior and Ace discharge anger rather than harbour it. Deprived of his property for a pittance by Curly, Ace never voices his misgivings about him in public; he simply rids himself of them by smashing a TV screen on which Curly is giving a commercial. Similarly, when Junior is warned by Curly against growing up like his father, he socks Curly on the jaw, sending him crashing through a window; after this, Junior does not bother to justify his actions to those around him, nor pursue the business any further.

Curly and his wife, Ruth, stand for the moderation and pragmatism that Peckinpah considers contemporary evils. Such appear to be the values of the future, too, since the Bonner children belong to Curly and his wife. The future for Curly's two small sons seems cruelly circumscribed, Junior's riding and Ace's wild schemes holding for the two boys a magic that their father's business interests never can. Filling the prairies with 'mobile homes', Curly exploits his Western heritage to make money. There is no redeeming cynicism to his behaviour as there is to that of Gil Westrum in *Ride the High Country;* Curly continually asserts the meaningfulness of his actions, even going so far as to claim that he is just trying to keep the family together. Ruth Bonner is a cold person; she and Curly seem little more than a team for making money. She is obsessed by notions of propriety, forbidding her mother-in-law to smoke before the baby and insisting her father-in-law buy her sons Coke instead of beer. Towards Junior, Ruth displays a revulsion so extreme it suggests that in a secret and suppressed way she may be attracted to him.

After Junior socks him on the jaw, Curly, always image-conscious, makes a big scene out of obtaining his revenge. He chooses the Palace Bar as his place, and after a show of muscle-flexing, he floors Junior, who nonchalantly picks himself up and talks quietly to Curly, unable to feel angry. Like the suit-clad types at the rodeo who flash money around and behave as big shots with the stars, Curly seems to be forever out to delude himself that wealth lends him some kind of virility. Underneath, however, he resents others for having the freedom he himself feels afraid to pursue. Through his denigration of Junior's riding, Curly contrasts sadly with Red Terwilliger, Junior's friend, fellow rodeo star, and respectful admirer. Curly's self-imposed role as head of the family is a further attempt to mask his inadequacies.

If, unlike Judd, Tyreen or the Wild Bunch, Junior lives in a world where even 'crashing out' is an impossibility, he does at least manage a final gesture of disaffiliation before leaving Prescott. Spending almost all of his prize money for riding Sunshine on a ticket to Australia for Ace and his dog, Junior commits economic suicide. As with Westrum's renunciation of a financial gain in favour of his allegiance to Judd in *Ride the High Country*, Junior is acknowledging another's right to pursue an elusive freedom. To Junior, it seems more sensible that his father should go to Australia for a wild time digging for gold and rearing sheep than that Curly should methodically devote himself to making a million dollars. By giving away his prize money, Junior is also making it clear that he rode Sunshine not for financial gain but for the experience of riding him – in a world where vitality is being squeezed out of life, where people are forced to compromise their dignity and their emotions, the kind of security money provides is useless; all that can finally matter, Junior triumphantly asserts, is catching what fragments of living remain.

But for Ali McGraw and a trashy music score, *The Getaway* could have been one of Peckinpah's finest achievements. Peckinpah almost conceals the severe limitations of McGraw's emotional range by his tacit recognition of them: the scene of her reconciliation with Steve McQueen in a garbage dump, for instance, is shot for much of the time with her face concealed by the frame of a derelict car in which she is hiding. Jerry Fielding originally wrote a score for the movie but McQueen had this scrapped – a pity since, if his work on Peckinpah's later and somewhat similar *Bring Me the Head of Alfredo Garcia* is anything to go by, Fielding's score probably underlined the man-woman relationship, according further centrality to McGraw's performance. The present score is made up mostly of grating harmonica music and makes the movie seem far colder than it actually is.

Despite these shortcomings, Carol McCoy remains one of Peckinpah's most admirably conceived woman characters, an equal to Hildy in *The Ballad of Cable Hogue*. In *The Getaway*, Peckinpah again tackles many of the preoccupations of *The Deadly Companions*, borrowing freely on the earlier movie – a scene where Doc McCoy slaps Carol recalls one where Yellowleg slaps Kit; McCoy briefly abandons Carol as Yellowleg does Kit; and in the climax McCoy kills a man who embodies the viciousness in his own personality as Peckinpah originally intended Yellowleg to do by having him kill Billy. In *The Getaway*, however, Peckinpah is able to bring the man-woman relationship to a worthwhile conclusion since he is not saddled with a straight-laced heroine. The film belongs, then, to that tradition in the American cinema – William Wellman's *Yellow Sky* and Nicholas Ray's *Party Girl* provide other examples – of movies that may begin by revealing a fascination with male aggression but end by evolving a faith in woman as a humanizing force.

The Getaway is a gangster movie, but it has similarities with Peckinpah's Westerns. Doc McCoy is a man out of his time, trying to assert an individualist ethic in a world where individual liberty is circumscribed. As in the Westerns also, the law proves morally ambiguous. McCoy is released from prison on the instigation of Benyon ('a man with political influence'), who wants him to rob a bank for him. Even though he is suspicious of the set-up surrounding the robbery, McCoy goes through with the robbery because he has a certain standard of ethics – 'When you make a deal, you're better off keeping up your end.' Benyon, however, is totally mercenary and unscrupulous and tries to arrange it so that McCoy does not come through alive.

The America across which McCoy and his wife flee from Benyon's henchmen is one characterized by indifference and inertia. The America of *The Getaway*, like that of *The Wild Bunch*, is at war, only this time none of the movie's characters are aware of this. Mostly unremarked, soldiers on their way to or from Vietnam are often seen in the background to the movie's main action. The media seem hardly ever to mention Vietnam, news bulletins on McCoy filling air-time after the robbery. Throughout, we are made aware of the appalling isolation of people from one another. During the final shoot-out in an El Paso hotel between McCoy and Benyon's henchmen, Peckinpah keeps cutting to other people in the hotel who appear but dimly aware of what is going on.

A key function of Rudy Butler, an accomplice of McCoy's in the robbery and eventually his pursuer, is to show how frontier vitality has become debased in the America of *The Getaway*; at one point, Peckinpah even links Butler with the spectacle of attacking Indians on a TV screen that has its volume turned down. Peckinpah also shoots Butler through the grill of one of vet Harold's animal cages, and on a number of occasions Butler reminds us of a caged animal, most memorably in the scene where he pelts Harold's wife, Fran, with food as Harold drives them along in his car. The extreme power and toughness of Butler leads us to believe he will play a decisive role in the action: but, as with Wolf Larsen in Jack London's *The Sea Wolf* and Dock Tobin in Anthony Mann's *Man of the West*, Butler is denied a sphere of action appropriate to him and reduced to acts of petty malice to discharge his energies. Butler's scenes with Harold and Fran do nothing to advance the main action of the movie; he spends much of his time teasing them, overeating or indulging in orgies with Fran.

McCoy's behaviour, however, is far from directionless – he is a force that seeks liberation. The movie's opening sequence – an interweaving of scenes of McCoy enduring the tedious ritual of prison life with flashbacks to his lovemaking with his wife – is given a frenzied close as McCoy is shown overturning a chessboard and smashing a matchstick bridge he has been constructing.

Even the world outside the prison appears in many ways like an extension of it: an assignation in a warehouse between McCoy and his confederates before the robbery is overlaid with noise similar to that of the prison's machine shop.

In the disorder after the robbery again the impression is of energy erupting. This disorder begins when Rudy Butler kills Jackson, a young thug who has panicked. As Butler shoots Jackson in the genitals, Peckinpah zooms out from an explosion that has been set off to create a diversion, exploiting the spectacle as an image to suggest the burning flush of genital sensation with which Jackson dies. Jackson's body falls from the car Butler is driving as birds take flight from a tree, giving a strange note of beauty to the scene. Meanwhile, McCoy and his wife are caught in traffic with another diversionary explosion timed to go off nearby. Reverting to the fury he displayed in prison, McCoy makes a dangerous manoeuvre across the road to turn around and ploughs into the wooden verandah of a house before he makes his escape. Especially since *Bullitt*, car chases, with their heavy wear and tear on cars, have become a fairly staple feature of American movies, thrown in just to give the audience a thrill. The car chases of *The Getaway*, however, are far from perfunctory. McCoy's rough handling of the cars he drives and his shooting at pursuing cars expresses his impulse to smash his way out of the modern technological society which traps him.

McCoy's wife is his one link with a harmonious world of instinct and emotion. In prison his recall of love-making with Carol provides him with a defence against the dehumanization of life there. These flashbacks to the love-making also give Doc's aggression against the chessboard and matchstick bridge a sexual dimension, making it appear at least partially an expression of frustration at the celibacy prison life has forced upon him. When he is released from prison, the first thing that McCoy does is to take a walk with his wife in a park. As he contemplates a river, he smiles for the first time in the film, and a sequence of shots of him and Carol bathing in the river in an harmonious dreamy pastoral precedes their return, dripping wet, to her apartment: they have, it seems, transformed McCoy's imaginings into a reality. But McCoy still remains tense: 'It does something to you,' he confesses about prison, before making love for the first time in four years.

Carol's motives in allowing herself to be seduced by Benyon are complex. On the one hand, she sleeps with Benyon because it is the only way she can finally persuade him to release McCoy. Yet, at the same time, she commits an act of willed infidelity as a reaction against the kind of man that prison is making of McCoy. The opening prison scenes end with a meeting between Carol and McCoy on visiting day. McCoy shows no emotion at all to her; she appears merely useful to him as an instrument for ensuring his release. Consequently, there is a double complicity.

Yet it is neither the deadening effect of prison nor the mercenary values of modern America that constitutes the greatest threat to McCoy's relationship with his wife: it is McCoy himself. Continually using a gun to display his masculinity, McCoy is clearly affected by the state of the society around him. In his authoritarian and possessive treatment of his wife, he appears only to be masking anxieties about her loyalty and his own right to her under the patriarchal shadow of Benyon. The conference McCoy holds before the robbery has a nightmare quality, Peckinpah stressing the mental strain under which McCoy lives. As McCoy outlines his plan, Carol stands by his side, appearing a fragile figure. McCoy is menaced on all sides: in a sarcastic gesture, Rudy Butler shines a torch in his face, and Benyon's second-in-command is revealed lurking in the background like the all-seeing power of Benyon.

When McCoy visits Benyon with the money after the robbery, the revelation of his wife's infidelity comes as the crystallization of his own inner fears. Carol shoots and kills Benyon to show she is on McCoy's side. Yet McCoy is unable to appreciate the true significance of her gesture; he just sees her as a betrayer. The scene ends with McCoy and Carol pointing their guns at each other, their love transformed into mutual hostility. As they drive away from Benyon's place, McCoy suddenly explodes with violence; driving his car off the road, he pulls Carol out and slaps her face.

Despite Carol's continual protestations of loyalty to him, McCoy is unable to see her infidelity as anything but a betrayal. Making a big show of caring only about money and himself, he seeks at once to punish her and to mask how deeply he has been hurt. When, at the railway terminus, she loses the bag containing the money, McCoy casually abandons her, catching a train he thinks the thief might be travelling on. When he retrieves the money, hours later, McCoy returns to her at the terminus where she has been waiting for him since he left. He has chosen to come back for her; yet he still refuses to show any emotion towards her, responding coldly when she embraces him.

Apart from illustrating the dissipation of frontier vitality, the Butler-Fran-Harold subplot provides a visual representation of McCoy's humiliation fears. The aggressive and virile Butler seems to be how McCoy would like to see himself. Butler at least has no problems with women; Fran is prompted to give herself to him as soon as she sees his gun. At the same time, Butler stands for McCoy's mental image of Benyon: an authority figure executing an exclusive right over woman. In this respect, McCoy is also Harold, the 'humiliated son' whom Butler and Fran bind up every night and force to watch their love-making. The link between McCoy and Harold is made visually explicit by Peckinpah: before she surrenders to Butler one evening, Fran menaces Harold with Butler's gun, and Peckinpah cuts to McCoy ambushed by police in a drive-in restaurant, making it appear as if McCoy himself is being menaced by Fran. When, subsequently, McCoy blows his top at the restaurant, it thus appears a consequence of his humiliation fears. McCoy tells Carol to drive off and they make a foolhardy escape, McCoy blasting gleefully away at the police who have become for him a surrogate target for aggression against authority and woman.

Pursued by the police, the McCoys take refuge in a garbage truck; and facing with his wife the thrashing metal limbs of the dark, mechanized interior of the truck, McCoy manages at last to comprehend that his relationship with his wife has enough potential to withstand the debilitating pressures of a hostile society. After the garbage truck sequence, Peckinpah returns to his subplot and reveals that Harold has committed suicide by hanging himself in a toilet. Harold's death appropriately corresponds to McCoy's release from anxiety. When they find themselves dumped on waste ground, this time it is Carol who wants to split up and McCoy who insists that they stick together. Moved by McCoy's final show of concern, Carol decides to stick with him after all and the two of them make their way to the highway through smoke clouds of burning garbage.

In the closing section of *The Getaway*, their relationship regains the warmth that characterized it during the earlier river scene. As their clothes are laundered, they share a cubicle together; in their hotel room at El Paso, they lie in one another's arms, no longer wary of each other as in previous hotel scenes.

In the first part of the film, McCoy coldly takes aim at the wounded and unconscious form of Butler in the shoot-out after the robbery. In the El Paso showdown, McCoy again has a chance to kill an unconscious Butler in cold blood, but this time he cannot bring himself to shoot. As McCoy and Carol flee the hotel, Butler fires and McCoy returns the fire, killing him in a fair fight without callousness. It is a final farewell to the anxiety that has prevented him from loving Carol. Butler's death is not a total renunciation of frontier vitality, as Doc Holliday's death signified for Wyatt Earp in *My Darling Clementine;* rather it affirms that the savage energy within McCoy has finally discovered a creative engagement through his relationship to his wife.

Largely on the grounds that he does not have his hero caught and punished, contemporary reviewers of *The Getaway* accused Peckinpah of pandering to a currently fashionable view of the criminal as hero. Yet Peckinpah was being consistent with attitudes he has expressed throughout his work. Like a true outlaw, Peckinpah has never cared much for the law; he has always been more concerned with what happens inside his heroes than whether they conform to any pre-existing standards of right and wrong. The issue at stake in *The Getaway* is not whether McCoy will recognize the error of his criminal ways, but whether he will be able to appreciate his wife's love for him, for only by appreciating this love can he affirm that his potential to stay human has not been destroyed.

McCoy and his wife are driven over the border into Mexico by an old cowboy, who reveals himself as a kindred spirit through the delight he takes in smashing his truck into cars. The old cowboy's friendliness makes a pleasant contrast to the nastiness and indifference of most of the people the McCoys have met on their flight. The cowboy does not condemn McCoy for living outside the law, and when he learns that McCoy and Carol are married, the cowboy begins to talk about his own wife, commenting that 'everything I am, I owe to her'. McCoy appears deeply moved by these words, silently acknowledging his own dependence on Carol. When they arrive in Mexico, McCoy tries to buy the cowboy's car for ten thousand dollars. The cowboy sticks out for twenty and a deal is finally struck when Carol insists that he deserves thirty. McCoy pays the cowboy the money, probably acquiescing to his wife's point of view for the first time in his life.

At the end of the movie, McCoy and Carol drive on into Mexico in the truck. We cannot be sure that they will ever find a place where their love is no longer threatened. Yet they have stuck together for a while, and in Peckinpah's world this counts for a great deal.

CHAPTER NINE: PAT GARRETT AND BILLY THE KID

> 'He who does not have confidence in that which is alive, or has lost it, easily falls prey to the subterranean fear of life which begets dictatorship. *That which is alive is in itself reasonable.* It becomes a caricature when it is not allowed to live.'
>
> Wilhelm Reich, *The Function of the Orgasm*

Historically, the action of *Pat Garrett and Billy the Kid* takes place before that of *The Wild Bunch.* Yet the West it depicts is in a more advanced state of paralysis than the earlier film. With its slow-motion solitary deaths, *Pat Garrett and Billy the Kid* presents a West where frontier vitality is in its dying embers. Whereas Harrigan, the authority figure in *The Wild Bunch*, was at times on hand to give his orders personally, Chisum, the cattle baron taking control of the West in *Pat Garrett*, remains aloof from the action and his wishes pass for law without anyone questioning them. *Pat Garrett*'s world is one of totally closed options: either the characters conform to the invincible will of Chisum or they are destroyed. Against this background Peckinpah examines how the 'buddy love' of the Western can be rooted in repression and coercion. The action of the movie centres on how the friendship of a particular male duo is pushed to an inevitable sadomasochistic conclusion: the ageing Pat Garrett seeks to survive at any cost, while Billy the Kid, his former sidekick, embraces destruction.

The Western has often seen the enforcement of law in terms of a repressive law versus the fraternal loyalty of male friendship. Robert Aldrich's *The Last Sunset*, Richard Thorpe's *Vengeance Valley* and *The Pistolero of Red River* – these adequate genre pictures and many other Westerns have dealt with the relationship between an unbalanced or antisocial protagonist and another who feels a brotherly friendship for him and yet is finally compelled to kill him in accordance with the patriarchal imperative of the culture in which they live. One of Anthony Mann's major achievements is his exploration of this dichotomy surrounding law enforcement, his heroes often subjected to neurotic stress through the clash between an allegiance to an outlaw past and a compulsion to enforce the law *(Bend of the River, Man of the West)*. *Pat Garrett and Billy the Kid*, however, is an all-out indictment of this kind of law-bringer as morally corrupt. Although he has ridden with Billy the Kid, Pat Garrett accepts a job as sheriff and kills his former friend in the name of the law. Ostensibly much more of a pragmatist than his Mann hero predecessors, Garrett claims he is just doing this to survive in changing times. But Garrett is deceiving himself when he thinks that he acts lucidly, for it is because of the disorientating impact of social forces that he betrays his friend.

Pat Garrett is played by James Coburn. The most striking feature of Coburn's screen *persona* has always been its self-reliance. Coburn achieved stardom in the late 'sixties by playing a string of characters whose audience appeal lay in the manner they treated women as objects for casual sex and always had the knack of making other men seem inferior in some way (the Flint films, *Waterhole 3*). Garrett is one of Coburn's best roles – it enables him to examine critically the narcissistic aspect of his screen *persona*. Garrett becomes obsessed with his own external appearance as a reaction against the loss of identity he secretly feels he has undergone through his allegiance to Chisum. In the scene in a barber's shop (a debased version of Earp's visit to a barber's shop in *My Darling Clementine*), Garrett gazes at himself in a mirror and insists his moustache be left on. Throughout the movie he appears to be taking great care over his clothes. Coburn brings just the right tone of arrogance to his performance to convey Garrett's growing self-absorption, yet he ensures that we never lose sight of the man whom Billy the Kid and the outlaws can still respect. As with his knife-thrower in *The Magnificent Seven* and Potts in *Major Dundee*, Coburn accords Garrett the dignity of the professional, so he towers above the minions of Chisum with whom he associates.

That we see less of the noble side of Garrett is the fault of the studio, who removed the movie's original opening. This apparently showed the murder of Garrett and made the rest of the movie appear as memory images flooding into the mind of the dying Garrett. Giving what some might consider a fanciful interpretation of historical facts, Peckinpah has spoken of the historical Garrett's death as follows: 'Garrett was killed by the so-called Santa Fe Ring, who hired him to kill Billy in the first place. It took place in White Sands, New Mexico, when Garrett, carrying his guilts and anger with him, apparently solved the murder of the Judge and his son [Colonel A.J.Fountain and his eight-year-old son, Henry, disappeared after Fountain had indicted several members of the Ring for the unlawful branding of cattle] and went against the Ring. The leader of the Ring was Albert Fall, who later became Secretary of the Interior.' The studio significantly changed the meaning of the movie by removing Peckinpah's interpretation of Garrett's death. Not only would this sequence have lent an added irony to Garrett's claims of being out to survive, it would likely have made Garrett a more characteristic Peckinpah protagonist. By squaring off against an emergent America that has destroyed his humanity, Garrett presumably asserted a belated claim to some kind of dignity. As it is, now all that we see is the Garrett who sells out to that America.

Garrett is always sarcastic to the 'poor company' with whom he works, thus attempting to blind himself to the degree to which he has sacrificed his autonomy as an individual. During a meeting arranged by Governor Lew Wallace, Garrett annoys the staid businessmen present by casting admiring glances at the cleavage of a Mexican waitress, and when the businessmen offer him money as an incentive to bring in Billy the Kid, Garrett's reply is admirably forthright: 'Stick it up your ass and burn it.' As he sets out after Billy, Garrett is joined by Poe, a deputy specially assigned to the case by Wallace. Poe hero-worships Chisum and – as if in consequence of this – feels disgusted by women. Draped in dark attire like Garrett, Poe represents what Garrett could become if he gave in totally to the forces that threaten his personality. Perhaps aware of this Garrett is singularly unpleasant towards Poe, brazenly allowing Poe to catch him whoring because he knows that this will disgust him. Garrett even goes so far as to defend Billy against Poe's disparaging remarks. Despite himself, Garrett cannot help feeling for Billy that loving admiration that Deke Thornton felt for Pike Bishop and Ford's Wyatt Earp felt for Doc Holliday.

Billy the Kid is increasingly romanticized by Peckinpah. In Billy's prison break in Lincoln, the notion of freedom is presented with a magical allure. Having despatched his guards, Billy sets about hacking off his chains singing aloud the names of the many places he has passed through; then in a carefree manner he rides through the onlookers in the streets and heads into the distance. Throughout the movie, shots of Billy's itinerant figure against some darkening skyline recur, lending a romantic dimension to Billy's rootlessness. Billy is also presented as a stud with women. When he returns to his outlaw friends after the prison break, he finds them all in bed with Mexican girls. One of them gives Billy his beautiful girl, as if acknowledging that Billy's sexual prowess gives him a prior claim on her. As Billy gets into bed with her, the other outlaws look on with approval.

Billy and his companions drift about forever on the edge of the civilization that is encroaching upon the frontier. Fowl are employed for their connotations of sexual prowess; as the movie opens, Billy and some friends are engaged in a chicken-shoot, luxuriating in the phallic power of one another's weaponry. Garrett suddenly arrives on the scene, having come to warn Billy to leave the territory, and he blasts away at a chicken with a shotgun, trying to show not so much that he is one of the boys but that he is top dog. Plagued by anxieties, Garrett takes every opportunity he can find to display his virility. When he later encounters a bargee shooting from his barge at bottles in a river, Garrett cannot resist blasting a bottle in an attempt to prove that he is better.

Since he is unable to discharge aggression against Chisum and his acolytes no matter how much they oppress him, Garrett is driven to channel this aggression more and more against the drifters and outlaws. At the beginning of the movie, he ambushes Billy and two other drifters without having any solid legal grounds for taking action against them. Later, Garrett rides his horse into a man and bullies him simply because he knows the man has a criminal record. Then, when he learns that Billy might be among a bunch of drifters nearby, he enlists the help of old Sheriff Baker and his wife, but when the three of them attack and kill the men, one of whom is Black Harris, an old friend of Garrett's, they find that Billy is nowhere to be seen. Later still, in a saloon-cum-store out in the wilds, Garrett encounters Alias, Holly and Beaver, three of Billy's friends, and sadistically bullies them.

Two scenes cut by the studio seem to have been particularly important for an understanding of Garrett's motivation, one between Garrett and his wife and the other between Garrett and Chisum. The wife was apparently Mexican and trying unsuccessfully to adapt to life in Lincoln where her husband was sheriff, while in the scene with Chisum Garrett revealed that Chisum had loaned him money to buy land. Presumably these scenes would have located Garrett's pursuit of Billy in terms of the evasion of woman and a guilt-laden filial piety. In the movie as it now stands, women are only of use to Garrett to bolster his butch behaviour. He takes on every prostitute in a bordello, having them all locked up afterwards as a final assertion of his power over them. He relies on force with women, having none of the natural command that Billy appears to have.

Pat Garrett's killing of Billy the Kid is one of Peckinpah's finest set pieces. Billy's preparations for love-making with a Mexican girl called Maria at old Pete Maxwell's place are intercut with the advance of Garrett and his accomplices through the night outside the house. By having the killing entail disturbing Billy's love-making, Peckinpah stresses the castrating nature of Garrett's violence. Garrett's dark figure slinking about the house reminds us of the dark avenger who stalked Pike Bishop's love-making in *The Wild Bunch.* While Garrett lingers upon the verandah, Billy exclaims 'Jesus' as he reaches orgasm with Maria – it is as if Billy realizes that enjoying an orgasm is sacrilege in the bourgeois-puritan culture in which he lives. Garrett broods upon the sounds of Billy's climax, seeming to project on Billy all his resentments and the sight of Garrett's subsequent firing at Billy's naked torso emphasizes the homosexual element to Garrett's sadism.

When in the Mann-Thorpe Westerns a protagonist with some form of social conscience kills his unbalanced 'brother', he appears implicitly to be killing a part of himself. Other Westerns have seen the enforcement of the law leading to a kind of self-castration for the enforcer. When Ethan Edwards kills Scar in Ford's *The Searchers* and Tom Doniphon kills Liberty Valance in *The Man Who Shot Liberty Valance,* they are by implication destroying all that is wild and vital in themselves; a marshal's killing of a fugitive Indian in Abraham Polonsky's *Tell Them Willie Boy Is Here* seems tantamount to the destruction of his capacity to love, the honest and open love affair between the Indian and his girl having been contrasted with the marshal's unsatisfactory relationship with a neurotic reservation worker. None of these Westerns, however, ends with as full a feeling of injustice as *Pat Garrett and Billy the Kid.* Garrett's killing of Black Harris, with whom he first rode into the territory; his forcing of Sheriff Kip McKinney to join him on his final expedition to repay favours he has done him in the past; his intrusion into the home of Pete Maxwell, who in richer and happier days, history tells us, gave Garrett his first real job in the territory – in a line of incidents, he betrays his frontier past, culminating in his killing of Billy. Garrett fires twice at Billy, his second shot – as history tells us – going astray. Peckinpah has this second shot hit a mirror. Mirrors sometimes splinter at moments of liberation for Peckinpah's characters; fittingly Garrett's mirror only cracks, revealing a distorted image of himself. When Poe knocks Maria from Billy's corpse and then tries to cut off his trigger finger, Garrett attacks him, realizing too late Poe is the right target for his aggression. Garrett destroys himself both emotionally and morally in killing Billy. As the movie's missing opening would probably have made clear, there is nothing left for him to do but to square off against the men who sent him on this errand.

While Peckinpah accords a romantic aura to his Billy the Kid, he also presents him in some psychological depth. This results in a serious flaw, since the romanticized Billy and the psychological Billy remain poles apart and are in no way reconciled by Peckinpah: in particular, Billy as male stud makes no sense psychologically. Many of the scenes involving Billy are flatly acted, Kris Kristofferson proving no match for James Coburn. Instead, it is largely from the movie's narrative drive and the expressiveness of Peckinpah's *mise en scène* that Billy derives his psychological depth.

'Wasn't long ago I was riding for Chisum and old Pat was an outlaw. The law's a funny thing, ain't it?' Billy comments in one of his rare moments of reflection and rationalization. Whereas Garrett takes a corrupt social set-up as an empirical basis for action, Billy is overwhelmed by a feeling of unreality when he contemplates the same set-up. Billy's friends seem equally unable to galvanize themselves into decisive action: it is hard for us to believe their claims after his escape that they were about to come to town to rescue him; and when bounty hunters later come after Billy, one of his friends even proves too busy eating beans to help. The death of Silva provides a solitary pointer to true solidarity amongst the frontier vagrants; surrounded by bounty hunters led by a dutiful negro of Chisum's, Silva allows himself to be gunned down rather than betray the whereabouts of Billy and Alias.

On one level, Billy appears committed to survival: during Garrett's ambush, he uses his wounded friend, Bowdre, to shield himself from gunfire; he shoots the amiable deputy, J.W.Bell, in the back to escape from Lincoln; and he kills Alamosa Bill, another deputy, by turning and firing at him before walking the agreed ten paces for their duel. But as Billy grows increasingly conscious of the legend that has grown around him, his attitude changes. Bob Dylan's deliberately colourless Alias, who has fled a job as printer in Lincoln to join Billy's drifters, is a constant reminder to Billy of how a whole way of life derives its only real sense of identity from the legend of Billy the Kid. When Billy asks

Alias what he thinks about his going to Mexico, Alias replies that 'it depends who you are'. Billy heads for Mexico all the same, but Alamosa Bill's dying words – 'Least I'll be remembered' – succeed in convincing Billy of the importance of the legend of Billy the Kid. When he decides to stay in the United States and face certain death, Billy is choosing to incarnate the legend foisted upon him, bearing witness through his individual defeat to the defeat of a whole way of life.

The landscape of the movie is composed mainly of vast and inhospitably empty plains, a fitting backdrop to a world where the maternal principle has no rights. After fighting with Garrett against the drifters, Sheriff Baker lies dying by a river in one such landscape, while his shotgun-toting wife sits watching him a short distance away, revealing an uncharacteristic show of womanly concern as tears begin to trickle down her cheeks. The scene is reminiscent in its desolation of Pike Bishop's scene with the Mexican girl before his death, Baker's relationship to his wife resembling that of a forlorn son to a concerned but somehow estranged mother. 'Momma put my guns in the ground. I can't shoot them anymore,' go the lines of Dylan's score, perfectly attuned to the mood of the scene.

The fascination with death in Billy the Kid is linked to the idea of exclusion from the mother. When Billy visits the trading-post for one of Mrs Horrell's meals, Chisum's authority is present in the form of Alamosa Bill to thwart his attempt to find domestic security for a brief time. As with Angel in *The Wild Bunch*, it is a woman who finally betrays Billy: although she feels affection for Billy, a prostitute tells Garrett of his whereabouts in submission to the superior authority that Garrett represents. As Billy nears the Mexican border, it is the spectacle of his gentle Mexican 'father', Paco, under attack that finally drives him back into the United States. As Paco lies dying, his daughter is raped by one of the attackers and it is to the sound of her baby crying in fear and bewilderment that Billy comes upon the ugly sight. As with Pike Bishop, a desire for death in Billy springs from a compulsion to respond passively to the patriarchal tyranny around him. During Garrett's ambush, Billy is fascinated by the sight of Bowdre being peppered by bullets, Bowdre reaching a point just before he dies where he can tell Billy that he no longer fears anything; and as the ambush ends, Billy stands before Garrett, his arms outstretched in a Christ-like gesture of martyrdom – it is as if Billy is awaiting the infliction of pain. Later, in the Lincoln gaol, when Billy is asked by Ollinger, Garrett's sternly religious deputy, to feel contrition for his past life, he responds with abuse, deliberately inviting Ollinger's wrath. Ollinger goes berserk. In a gesture suggestive of fellatio, he rams his shotgun in Billy's chest. Yet still Billy remains unrepentant, inviting violence.

The sexual imagery of Billy's killing underlines his female dependence on Garrett in his friendship towards him. Billy's last orgasm can be seen as a sacrilege in terms of his psychology because of the link between sex and punishment the *mise en scène* implies to be haunting the character. Yet there is a quality of mutiny to Billy's final submission to Garrett's bullet. Garrett seeks to hide from himself the manner in which an oppressive patriarchy has defiled him. Billy, on the other hand, finally openly assumes a female role and thus acknowledges the working of that tyranny.

Yet, Peckinpah seems to consider that there is too much resignation about Billy's death for it to provide a fitting climax, and he works hard to inject more defiance into the closing scenes. To this effect, Peckinpah himself appears as a coffin-maker, to reject indignantly the offer of a drink from Garrett. Also, when Garrett fires at Billy, Peckinpah cuts away briefly to a friend of Billy's called Eno, who leaps from a house, gun in hand. A little earlier, Eno has suggested to Billy that the drifters and outlaws band together as a fighting force under Billy's leadership; and, by this shot of Eno ready for action, Peckinpah appears to be lamenting Billy's inability to follow his friend's suggestion. In the closing scene, Alias, Eno and Billy's other friends sit staring maliciously at Garrett as he rides away. A defiant small boy hurls a sod of earth at Garrett, contrasting with an earlier boy who dutifully ran errands for Garrett. Even if you can never win, Peckinpah is telling his audience, this is no excuse not to stare the meaningless reality of things in the face.

'The prophecy was that I would be dismembered; and – Aye! I lost this leg. I now prophesy that I will dismember my dismemberer. Now then, be the prophet and fulfiller one.'

'But thou art but my fiery father; my sweet mother, I know not. O cruel! What hast thou done with her.'

Ahab in Melville's *Moby Dick*

Bring Me the Head of Alfredo Garcia is a major work in terms of Peckinpah's obsequies for the crucified sons of America. The most Gothic of all Peckinpah's movies, it is a sombre examination of the death-wish mentality that has haunted the director. The dutiful son who must become a law-giving father, woman as mother and whore, money as compensation for sexual failure – despite the diffuseness of its dream-like setting, *Alfredo Garcia* succinctly exposes contradictions underlying Peckinpah's work and the American Dream.

As *Bring Me the Head of Alfredo Garcia* opens, a pregnant Mexican girl is escorted by two men from a sunlit riverside setting to the dark and oppressive court of her father, a Mexican patriarch called El Jefe. As she is tortured on her father's orders before the whole court, her mother looks on with a strange kind of impassivity. Eventually the girl is no longer able to withstand the torture and cries out the name of the man who impregnated her – 'Alfredo Garcia'. Decapitation being a traditional Mexican way of taking revenge, El Jefe offers a million dollars for Alfredo's head to Max and Frank, two American hoods, who are on hand. The action moves through a sequence of journeys by car and plane to Mexico City. But we are not moving into a totally different world; rather the patriarchal court of El Jefe is concealed beneath the trappings of the modern world. The natural sacredness of a pregnant young girl and her father's unnatural insistence on the inviolability of her chastity – these are the poles around which the drama of the movie will evolve.

In Peckinpah's movies, the tangible world often has the function of giving form to the demons that madden the characters: in *Major Dundee*, for instance, the Apache are not only envisaged as a castrating force by certain of the characters, they actually become 'castrators' when they wound Dundee. *Alfredo Garcia* is even more of a psychodrama than Peckinpah's other movies, its characters all implicated in the hero's tormented psyche. We first encounter Bennie, the American drifter hero, in a Mexico City bar filled with American tourists. Who is Bennie? Why does he alone respond to Quill and Sappensly, two associates of Max and Frank, when they ask after Alfredo Garcia? The only way we can answer these questions is by taking the opening of the movie as a mirror of Bennie's psyche. Peckinpah himself suggests we do this: Alfredo, as is later revealed, has already been killed in a car crash, and while Bennie talks to Quill and Sappensly, Peckinpah overlays a shot of his hero's face with the noise of a car crashing, thus implying that Bennie's fate is linked with that of Alfredo. 'He was like a son to me', El Jefe says of Alfredo, implying he has committed something equal to incest with his daughter; and, indeed, Bennie's compulsive desire to help Quill and Sappensly suggests he somehow mysteriously fears contagion from El Jefe's curse.

When Bennie, dressed in a clean suit, goes to visit Max's gang to tell them he can bring them the head, his behaviour has the quality of forced filial piety; Bennie even allows himself to be hectored into accepting a paltry two hundred dollar advance for his services. The nightmarishness that the meeting has for Bennie is made clear when Quill insists that Bennie remove his sunglasses to have his photograph taken: as the flashlight lights up Bennie's face, he shudders as if pierced by some penetrating stare. Bennie is too intimidated by the gang to realize that they are also in flight from anxieties – Max by dominating women, Frank by caring only about money, Quill and Sappensly by using 'buddy love' as a bastion against the complications of women.

Bennie is tormented by the discovery that Elita, his singer-prostitute girlfriend, has slept with Alfredo. Not only is he disgusted she has enjoyed sex with another man; he feels himself humiliated to have, however temporarily, lost a woman to another man. Securing Alfredo's head seems increasingly to Bennie to provide a way out of this dilemma. Like Max's gang, he comes to seek invulnerability through power and money.

Although the scene in no way advances the narrative, a nocturnal encounter Bennie and Elita have with two hippies succinctly clarifies Bennie's torment. As one holds Bennie at gunpoint, the other leads Elita away, slaps her face and cuts her sweater, only mysteriously to withdraw and sit down. Elita advances towards the hippie as if he has an exclusive right over her, only to reach out to him finally with a kind of maternal tenderness. As with Angel in *The Wild Bunch* and Sumner in *Straw Dogs*, Bennie spirals into violence at the moment another man takes his woman. Having eluded his hippie captor, Bennie charges forth, coming to stand before a backdrop of grass and rocks previously graced by Elita: a gun in his hand and anger on his face, he appears an intruder amid the natural harmony about Elita and the hippie as they embrace. Bennie guns down the hippie in a rage of disgust and, as his aggression implies, of envy. Finally he reduces Elita to tears breaking the news to her she is to help him violate Alfredo's grave.

At the beginning of the movie, Bennie's behaviour appears as unpleasantly butch as that of Pat Garrett earlier. Bennie is bossy with the Mexicans who work in the bar he part owns, and when he meets an old friend at the hotel where Elita works, he is so aggressive in his display of friendship that he offends the man.

But as the movie progresses, Bennie emerges as an increasingly tragic figure. Despite all the perverse motives bound up with the journey, he reveals at times that in taking Elita away with him he genuinely desires to find a place where her love might reach him. It is perhaps not a coincidence that for the first stages of their journey Peckinpah should use a series of dissolves as he did for the river idyll opening, for Bennie and Elita's love must be just as cruelly destroyed as the idyll was, Bennie unable to elude the nightmare descending upon him.

As they picnic beneath a tree, Bennie begins to tell Elita about himself: 'Hell, I've never been any place I'd like to go back to. That's for damn sure.' She tells him of a beautiful Spanish town she once knew, but when asked who she was with there, she refuses to reply – perhaps it was Alfredo Garcia. 'I want to go some place new', Bennie exclaims; then, noticing two of Max's henchmen passing in a car, he forces Elita to drink a toast to Alfredo as a rebuke to their prying eyes. He even talks of marrying her, but cannot propose to her properly.

Bennie's inability to choose between love and violence is underlined by his attachment to his gun, the weapon a legacy from army days. In a hotel room, we see Bennie first seated on a bed loading his gun and then moving to the shower where Elita is. Contemplating Elita's wet and naked body, Bennie tells her that he loves her. His words, however, are spoken with an air of complete unreality; certainly they are not meant as a prelude to love-making. Perhaps Bennie's most overt show of loyalty towards Elita comes when he unleashes his aggression against a hotel manager who refuses them a room on the grounds that they are not married. Elita is moved by Bennie's display of love for her by attacking a man who would denigrate her and she insists that she and Bennie be given the best room in the house.

Elita has a strength of character that Bennie lacks; she has no inhibitions about love-making, and when Bennie shuts himself away alone in his little room to hatch his schemes, she enters in the dead of night to climb into his bed. The next morning, Elita lies around naked on the bed, having no qualms about her appearance. Bennie makes a comic contrast: after waking to find himself plagued by pubic lice, he wraps himself in his dressing-gown and dons his habitual sunglasses. Elita has loved Alfredo but she also loves Bennie, and she goes with Bennie to the grave not out of any desire for money but because of this love for him.

They dig up Alfredo's grave, but as Bennie stands in the grave, his machete poised ready to decapitate the corpse, someone knocks him unconscious. When Bennie regains consciousness, he finds himself buried in the grave with Elita dead at his side. Bennie begins to chide the corpse, but gradually comes to understand the truth. He curses the eyes of Mexicans who come upon him. Yet as he drives away, it is the eyes of El Jefe's henchmen that Bennie curses, his demented mind finally focussing on his true oppressors. Bennie catches up with the two henchmen who were the attackers at Alfredo's grave, kills them, and takes the head from the car. Then, as if some magical power flows into him from the head, he walks over to the corpse of one of the men and fires more shots into it 'because it feels so damned good'. The violence in Bennie, finally directed against true oppressors, is now able to find catharsis.

The spectacle of Bennie leading American tourists in the singing of a song from the Mexican Revolution at the beginning of the movie emphasizes his remoteness from the Mexican people amongst whom he has chosen to live. But through his loyalty to Alfredo's head, Bennie finally achieves some empathy with these people; he is pursued by Grandmother Moreno and her clan, who are out to protect Alfredo's dignity by retrieving the head. When they corner him, Bennie casts all his money aside to show *dinero* no longer provides a motivation for his actions. Earlier, Alfredo's grandmother has shown contempt for Bennie, objecting to him paying his respects at her grandson's grave, but now she and her clan hesitate before him, vaguely respectful of someone who like themselves can place a personal code of honour above all else. Yet they still persist in trying to take the head, and when all seems lost, Quill and Sappensly arrive. A battle ensues, the henchmen of the 'father' massacring the 'mother' and her clan, all except for an old man.

Haunted by memories of his lost love and with no one at all close to him, Bennie becomes the loneliest of all Peckinpah's lonely heroes. Yet Alfredo's head does provide him with some comfort. As Bennie drives on, he talks to it; far more solidly than Dundee and Sumner ever managed with their respective espousals of flag and village idiot, Bennie comes finally to accept an Oedipal destiny through his allegiance to the head. Yet before this is possible he must first become the law-giver. The shroud of nightmare about Bennie seems to lift as Max and his gang reveal themselves to be pathetically vulnerable in death. As Bennie, in his revenge, becomes a manic travesty of the father, each of these men seems to disintegrate before him: 'Johnny', Sappensly calls out to his beloved and dying Quill before he dies, and Max and Frank panic when Bennie brandishes his gun and refuses to take their money, Max eagerly giving Bennie El Jefe's address.

As Bennie finally arrives at his court El Jefe is doting over Alfredo's son as the child is baptized, the child's mother and grandmother looking on, in exclusion. Festivities for the baptism, among which Bennie cuts a melancholy figure, inject a mood of rebirth into the movie's close, Peckinpah cutting between the head Bennie is carrying and the baby about to be baptized. Leading Bennie away from the throng, El Jefe offers him the million dollars for the head. Bennie rejects the offer; he must have his revenge, for nothing is able to compensate him for the symbolic obliteration of his phallic identity and the death of the woman he might have loved. He explodes with violence against El Jefe's minions; then the girl comes to his side, now holding Alfredo's son, and at her instigation he turns the gun on El Jefe. Openly challenging El Jefe's incest-curse, Bennie returns to the girl a medallion bearing Alfredo's picture that Max took from her at the movie's opening.

But Bennie remains trapped by himself; like Steve Judd, he finds it easier to die for woman than to commune with her. 'You take care of the son and I'll take care of the father,' Bennie says to the girl as he leaves with the head, and she with the child. As Bennie drives away, Peckinpah cuts back to a small boy fumbling with the gun of one of El Jefe's dead minions and then wandering forlornly around the ancestral home: the scene provides proleptically an epitaph for Bennie. Like other Peckinpah heroes, Bennie finds in the passive submission to gunfire a release for his libido and an escape from the cruel burden of having felt compelled to become the law-giver. Pursued by more of El Jefe's minions, Bennie dies riddled with bullets with the head by his side. As a gun turns its annihilating fire on the audience, the frame freezes, Peckinpah leaving his audience to emerge from the experience like Ishmaels buoyed-up from the vortex. *Bring Me the Head of Alfredo Garcia* finally becomes an outcry for a world where the heart and not the head holds sway, where the kind of authority that ruins its hero can no longer exist.

CHAPTER ELEVEN: THE KILLER ELITE

> 'How I snuffed that Tartar air! – and how I spurned that turnpike earth! – that common highway all over dented with the marks of slavish heels and hoofs; and turned me to admire the magnanimity of the sea which will permit no records.'
>
> Ishmael in *Moby Dick*

So often in Peckinpah's movies the judge is destroyed along with those on whom he passes verdict. The desire to become the law that has so often overwhelmed the Western hero, just as it overwhelmed Henry King's Tol'able David, Peckinpah has generally seen as leading to death. Except for Sumner in *Straw Dogs*, all of his heroes are destroyed when they try to stand for a repressive law. If in *Ride the High Country* Steve Judd begins as a character something like Ford's Wyatt Earp, he ends, like Ford's Doc Holliday, dissolving his personality in death because he feels too oppressed to continue to face life. Like Judd, Major Dundee and Pat Garrett, other Peckinpah law-givers, would have found death but for changes and cuts made by producers. Those Peckinpah heroes who become the law for the pleasure of destroying the law are also finally propelled towards death as a gateway to humility; for, like Melville's Ahab, they can only become the images of everything they hate: both Bennie and Pike Bishop are condemned to live as exiles, ranting and raving against an isolation that is actually the consequence of their own obsession with power. All of those Peckinpah heroes who find some kind of inner harmony reject the blandishments of power completely. Despite Hemingwayesque undertones, *Junior Bonner* primarily celebrates the humility of its hero's response to life. Both Doc McCoy and Cable Hogue come to acknowledge that the most important thing in life is to care for someone; and in that they finally abandon all desire to revenge injuries done to them, they achieve the renunciation of power that other Peckinpah heroes can only embrace in the paroxysm of violence. Against a stern law that subjugates all life, Peckinpah continually sets an individual morality that has its base in no one presuming to set himself up in judgement on another. If freedom is the absence of repression, then it is contingent on each individual struggling against becoming an agent for repression himself.

Central to the director's attitude to power has always been the way he treats wounding. If wounding can have a drastically repressive effect on his characters, it can also be positive since it may remind them that they no longer need bear the burden of embodying the law: it is only after a wounding that Major Dundee discovers comradeship with his men. If so many of Peckinpah's heroes find a joy in dying violently, it is because this provides them with a release from their anxieties: they come at last to understand that it is better to be pierced by the father's stare than to become the father. Even more than *The Ballad of Cable Hogue* and *The Getaway*, *The Killer Elite* is concerned with how a man can find inner harmony; it is Peckinpah's love-song to the wound as a symbol of humility.

The Killer Elite again finds Peckinpah examining his hero's anguish in a political perspective. On one level, the movie is a criticism of the CIA. It opens with a quote from Lawrence Weyburn, head of Com-Teg (a private company that does work for the CIA); Weyburn is refusing to acknowledge the existence of special departments like Com-Teg. For the movie's credit sequence, mysterious hands appear putting explosives in place and a bird is seen feeding its young while the noise of children at play off-screen is heard. An ensuing explosion, the work of Com-Teg agents, draws together these disparate strands into a representation of the devious paternalism of the CIA and its special departments.

The Killer Elite is a movie totally against power, not just attacking authority in the form of lofty figureheads like Weyburn but all the minions who are in the service of such authority – the ridiculous compulsion of the average person to project an image of authority is satirized in a comedy sequence concerning a policeman who pulls up the car of the movie's hero, Mike Locken, only to find that there is a bomb attached to the vehicle.

'My father was a minister. That's what he always wanted me to be'; these lines of Weyburn's are crucial to an understanding of the movie, for what Peckinpah hates about organizations like the CIA and Com-Teg is that they are a consequence of America's puritan ancestry, the product of a blind desire to subjugate and control.

In many ways *The Killer Elite* recalls a Western. After the explosion that ends the credit titles, Peckinpah introduces us to Mike Locken and George Hansen, two Com-Teg agents helping a defector to escape; and the first part of the movie deals with the friendship of these two men, modern and sinister versions of Cooper's Leatherstocking and Chingachgook. Finally betrayed and wounded by Hansen, Locken must become an avenger: it is the type of plot that has been more used in Westerns than crime thrillers, yet in Peckinpah's hands it is subjected to an extraordinarily enlightened treatment.

Mike Locken is played by James Caan, an important actor in terms of the American cinema's fascination with toughness. The Caan *persona* is one of aggressive virility, often with hints of homosexuality (notably in *The Godfather* and *The Gambler*). It is not surprising, therefore, that Howard Hawks should have played a large part in launching Caan's career. In Hawks' *Red Line 7000* Caan plays a racing driver who nurtures a deep and fearful envy for the boss of his team and is plunged into dementia when he falls in love with the boss's ex-girlfriend. Predictably, Hawks proved unable to plumb the neurotic depths of the Caan *persona*, and in his next film, *El Dorado*, relegated Caan to the less problematic role of a Hawksian young gun.

In *The Killer Elite* Peckinpah proves particularly responsive to the exigencies of the Caan *persona*. Locken's desire to demonstrate physical prowess is located early in the movie as a consequence of anxieties about women when at a party he tries to impress an elegant woman by doing press-ups before her. Though domineering with women, Locken allows his life to be totally regulated and controlled by Hansen; he even lets Hansen look after his money. Like *Pat Garrett and Billy the Kid*, *The Killer Elite* examines the familiar 'buddy love' of the American cinema with the intention of finally criticizing it; bound up with Locken's dependence on Hansen, as with Billy the Kid's on Garrett, is a female passivity.

Robert Duvall's Hansen is a relative of *Cable Hogue*'s Joshua and of Pat Garrett; like them, he needs to dominate a friend so as to deceive himself that he is not controlled by the society in which he lives. Hansen remains aloof from women – Peckinpah stresses this during a stripclub rendezvous of Hansen's by cutting between him and a stripper of whom he is totally oblivious. Locken's sex life nauseates Hansen. He watches with disdain as Locken does press-ups before the woman at the party; and then at five in the morning he bursts into the bedroom where Locken has been making love, reminding Locken that company business necessitates their departure. As the two buddies drive away, Hansen plays his trump card. Having gone through the woman's handbag, he has discovered a doctor's note stating she has a vaginal infection and he embarrasses Locken by threatening to make this information known to everyone they know.

Yet Hansen has sold out to the other side and the surface calm of their friendship is finally shattered by gunfire. Hansen kills Vorodny, the defector they are transporting, and then wounds Locken in arm and leg. As with Pat Garrett's killing of Billy the Kid, Hansen's wounding of Locken is given an erotic charge, Locken shot as he emerges from the shower. Like Garrett's, Hansen's motives run deeper than simply betrayal for financial security: the shooting for Hansen is the enactment of a dark love, the release of a libido that is denied access to woman. Like so many psychopathic protagonists in the American cinema – Cody Jarrett in Walsh's *White Heat* or Emerson Cole in Mann's *Bend of the River* – Hansen seems to crave beneath his aggressiveness to be wounded himself, deliberately not finishing off Locken when he surely knows that Locken will want his revenge.

'The scar looks beautiful', Locken is told by a doctor who patches up his wounds. Yet to Locken the wounding has come as a nightmare revelation of an emasculated powerlessness. A season in hell is sealed when Lawrence Weyburn and his area supervisor, Cap Collis, explain to him that he is no longer their number one boy since the wound has crippled him. Recovered but still having to wear callipers, Locken responds to the situation in the only way he knows – by seeking to demonstrate virility. He takes up martial arts, but this cannot relieve his anxieties. During one of Locken's work-out sessions, Collis turns up to remind him menacingly of his being a cripple.

Locken takes up home with Amy, a nurse who has looked after him in hospital. There is no sexual vitality about their relationship. His main concern is with recovering from his wounds and his relationship to Amy thus largely recalls that of an infant to its mother. Yet there is a positiveness about Amy's role, particularly when we compare her to many of the female characters in Peckinpah's earlier movies. She stands as indelibly as a source of love as the mother of Alfredo's child was by the end of *Alfredo Garcia*. Amy only ever looks upon Locken with compassion and thus stands in opposition to the prying eyes of Weyburn's world.

Weyburn condescends to give Locken a chance to prove himself a man again and designates to him the job of protecting Yuen Chung, an exiled Formosan patriot on his way back home. Locken will go up against a group of international assassins – the Killer Elite – and George Hansen. With news of Weyburn's offer, Collis invades the boat-house of Locken and Amy. Locken warms to going up against Hansen; the journey to war is on again, and women can wait. Yet for all its mutedness, Locken's parting from Amy is deeply moving. When Peckinpah frames the earnest discussion of Collis and Locken from a space in the room vacated by Amy, he seems to be mourning the manner she can be frozen only into the familiar ritual of lovelessness. Throughout the movie Peckinpah uses the sea of its San Francisco setting as a symbol for a benevolent and harmonious nature, and the sea takes on a particular significance in relation to Amy, her taking of Locken to live by the sea coming as an indication that she has begun the lifting of the veil of pain that separates him from others.

Able to choose his own men for the mission, Locken enlists the aid of Mac and Miller, two old friends. Miller is played by Bo Hopkins in a manner that recalls his roles as Crazy Lee in *The Wild Bunch* and Frank Jackson in *The Getaway*. When we are first introduced to Miller, he is shooting clay pigeons on a promontory overlooking the sea, seemingly oblivious to the natural splendour about him. Like Locken himself, Miller is a man cut off from the world: he can conceive of birth and death only as a process of unspeakable cruelty, devotion to a cult of violence providing his main reason for living. Miller is dismissed as a 'psycho' by Com-Teg, yet his demented hatred of all authority takes on a strange validity when during a shoot-out in San Francisco's Chinatown he guns down a policeman; on examination the policeman is revealed to be an imposter, one of the enemy in disguise.

Mac and Miller reflect tensions in Locken's psyche. If Miller stands for the side of Locken in demented revolt, Mac is an extension of the soothing force emanating from Amy.

Mac is one of the great figures of Peckinpah's cinema. Physically Burt Young recalls Ernest Borgnine in *The Wild Bunch*, yet his Mac is a more balanced person than Borgnine's Dutch. Mac's attitude towards life is one of complete humility – his fidgety gesture of removing his hat, one of the many inventive elements in Young's performance, repeatedly underlines this attitude. Mac exists as a reminder that self-respect is in no way proportional to power or political position. Mac has given up working for Com-Teg and now runs a garage – 'I used to think what I did was nice and necessary, you know.' His main motive in joining Locken on the mission is friendship. Throughout the mission, Mac criticizes Locken's revenge motive against Hansen, particularly the way Locken uses Yuen Chung and his party as bait to trap Hansen. During the Chinatown shootout, Mac prevents Locken from staging an insane showdown with Hansen by refusing to drive away Chung in his taxi until Locken joins them.

Mac's friendship for Locken has nothing in common with Hansen's; and even more devastatingly than the Westrum-Judd relationship in *Ride the High Country*, the Mac-Locken relationship in *The Killer Elite* is a refutation of the need of Hawksian professionalism to prove 'good enough'. Locken fears Mac's friendship for the same reason that he fears Amy's love – because it is completely spontaneous and does not ask him to be anything he is not. When Mac visits him in hospital, Locken will not see him. Locken finds it easier to put on a manly show before Weyburn and Collis than to relax before his old friend. Yet as the mission progresses, Locken warms to Mac. Mac's relationship with Miller parallels his relationship with Locken. Mac tries to prevail upon Miller to curb his homicidal tendencies and forces him into friendship by insisting on calling him by his first name – 'Jerome'.

The Killer Elite seems a critique of the excesses of Peckinpah's previous work. This may be conscious on Peckinpah's part. Peckinpah may have chosen to call the nurse Amy as a rejection of the misogyny surrounding the Amy of *Straw Dogs*. Certainly the movie as a whole totally contradicts the narrow morality of *Straw Dogs*. Where Sumner fights the villagers to defend *his* house, Locken is forced by Mac to confront this kind of showdown as merely a symptom of a particular social set-up. As they hide from Hansen at night in San Francisco's dock area, Mac attacks Locken for being so obsessed with personal injuries that he cannot see Hansen's betrayal in a political perspective – 'They're all trying to hurt you, Mike, all the goddam power systems.' When, having captured Chung's daughter, Hansen lures Locken into a confrontation, it is to confirm the truth of Mac's words. Revealing himself as just a tool of a particular power system, Hansen explains that he is in the pay of Collis, who is playing everyone off against each other. When Hansen offers Locken money to help him in killing Chung, Locken's response is just to walk away. He no longer feels compelled to play a tough guy role; he will submit to Hansen's gunfire if Hansen is low enough to pull the trigger.

Miller takes advantage of Hansen being put off guard and kills him; and as Locken contemplates the crumpled corpse of Hansen, he seems to acknowledge the futility of the death towards which the destructive part of his own personality has been propelling him. Yet Locken falls prey to one last spasm of mad rage and strikes Miller, only to apologize to him afterwards. He now seems not only to be liberated from the perverse control Hansen had over him, but also to have achieved some objectivity towards the revenger in himself.

In its narrative rhythm, *The Killer Elite* creates the impression of a machine breaking down in submission to a world of natural and spontaneous harmonies. Peckinpah intercuts a scene in Weyburn's office with the liberating slow-motion of the assassins' attack on Chung at San Francisco airport, and another office scene is intercut with Locken sailing out to sea. Locken's encounter with the assassins, the movie's final sequence, takes place in San Francisco's Suisun Bay, on board one of a fleet of warships anchored there, and, following the nocturnal death of Hansen, this sun-drenched seascape comes as an assertion of the natural world.

In the final fight with the assassins, Miller becomes a man in search of death and dies emptying the contents of his gun into the assailant who kills him. A child of the long night that ended with Hansen's death, Miller does not belong in the new dawn that is opening up: all that is left for him is for the violence to come on forever. Yet Miller's death can go on unmourned since by dying he atones for his vengeance against Hansen and thus through him the self-consuming hatred in Locken can find its catharsis. Moreover, it does not appear as if the dreadful fury in Miller has simply been extinguished by death; rather, it is as if this fury has been subsumed into the sunlit world about him.

During the fight with the assassins, Peckinpah moves his audience through an involvement with violence to a total distanciation from it. As the group make ready to board the warship, Peckinpah often frames Locken with Miller, but during the fight Miller becomes separated from Locken, going off to die alone. Locken is finally seen fighting by the side of Mac, the two men using any trick they can to survive. We glimpse the assassins scurrying about the warship: dressed in grey, they seem part of the ship's metal. Like the French in Major Dundee, they represent the mindless professionalism to which the movie's hero has aspired; and, as with Dundee and his men, it is by not playing the game that Locken comes through the fight. Being a 'cripple' involves no handicap, his walking stick proving a useful weapon and giving him an advantage over his opponents. The fight ends as Yuen Chung responds in a showily heroic way to a challenge to a Samurai confrontation with one of the assassins. 'Some things you can't push away' – this scene is very close to a Western showdown. Possibly Peckinpah sees himself as making a sort of critique on the stand of Sumner in *Straw Dogs*. Certainly Yuen Chung's action seems of little value, even though he kills the assassin.

In *The Killer Elite*, the 'castrating father' does not exist as one monstrous single figure, but he is broken down into three figures. If the confrontation with Hansen provides an important stage in Locken's moral development, it is meetings with Collis and Weyburn that enable Locken to achieve full liberation. Before the final fight, Locken meets Collis, who offers him Hansen's job. Locken's response is to shoot Collis in the arm and the leg, the fate that Collis dealt out to him through Hansen. This gesture comes as further evidence of Locken's awareness of the workings of the power system around him. Boarding the ship after the fight, Weyburn takes charge of Yuen Chung; and Locken realizes that all the time he has been responsible to Weyburn rather than for Chung. Perhaps by the same token, he also realizes that he failed in his responsibility for Vorodny earlier. Weyburn offers Locken Collis' job, but Locken rejects the offer and walks past Weyburn with Mac, the two friends sailing away on Collis' yacht. Now a sad and lonely figure, Weyburn looks after them.

In *The Killer Elite*, Peckinpah again recalls the Melville of *Moby Dick*. In its *dénouement*, *Moby Dick* can be seen as a critique of the male duo that has become a convention of American narrative as a legacy from Cooper's Leatherstocking tales. Here, after the mad Captain Ahab dies in pursuit of the White Whale, Ishmael, his passive accomplice, is set forth to seek out a new world. Similarly, *The Killer Elite* contrasts with Westerns like *The Searchers* and *Winchester '73* in that it has the dominant partner of the male duo killed off and puts forward the sensibility of the wifely confederate as being the one of greatest moral value. In this movie, the terror of being female that has so haunted the male protagonists of *Pat Garrett* and *Alfredo Garcia* is completely banished; for, after Hansen's death, Locken overcomes all terror towards the female component in his own personality. His wounding, even if it has been for him the revelation of his emasculation, comes no longer to oppress him. As Locken heads away with Mac, Mac is worried about a woman he is leaving behind and Locken tells him not to worry about her. Here, Locken's rejection of women is more positive than his abandonment of Amy in favour of a journey to war, for it now seems that, unlike a number of Peckinpah's previous protagonists, he can no longer be bothered to use women to demonstrate a bogus virility, a surly relationship with Chung's young daughter having come as a last attempt on his part to play at being something he is not. In *The Killer Elite*, Peckinpah completely rejects the respect for an aggressive masculinity that so many American directors have sought to express through their heroes; instead, he chooses to extol the virtue of the human psyche in all its contingencies.

Locken may not know where he is heading at the end of the movie, but this is not important, for he has rejected the past: unlike Weyburn, he does not need to subjugate or own anyone or anything to define an identity. He has come to understand that all along the sickness was in himself and the society that produced him but it was never in the world. Locken finally rejects a whole way of life geared towards death, experiencing a oneness with the world which Steve Judd could only feel when he looked up on the high country for the last time and which Pike Bishop felt all too briefly during his dying orgasm. When Locken sails from the warship he does so acknowledging that, as for everyone else who is living and will live, a place in the world is his inalienable birthright. He goes forward to receive the world into himself, to be wounded all over again. *The Killer Elite* ends with all terrors banished, its director endorsing a response to life that is totally and lastingly erotic. Life is desire – this is the simple truth that fractures a whole society founded upon the anguish of false renunciation.

> 'I have experienced violence but nothing has hurt me as much as being in love.'
>
> Sam Peckinpah

So much of Peckinpah's work deals with a journey through hell, a journey where a psychopathic anti-authoritarianism is transformed into a moral philosophy. The individual is given back custody of his inner drives through their violent unleashing, and this becomes a corrective to a society that suppresses, both physically and sexually, any individuality that challenges its monolithic authority. The individual fights to reassume his place at the centre of the scheme of things, and to shoulder a responsibility that the state seeks to take from him on all sides. He also seeks to feel at one with himself and the world about him – the world, that is, beyond the reach of the authoritarianism of the state, where there are forces fully vibrant and alive, warm and good.

For all their surface jingoism, movies like Walsh's *Objective Burma* and Fuller's *Merrill's Marauders* are largely about the masochism of men who, after submitting to the harsh pragmatism of war, become driven on just for the experience of it. It is because *Cross of Iron* is a war movie that it proves a so much more congenial vehicle for Peckinpah to transpose his concerns to non-American soil than *Straw Dogs*. If the topic of the disintegration of the Nazi army gives the director ample opportunity to continue his denunciation of the army as one of the lowest forms of human society, it also encourages him to respond to his fascination with the purgative dynamism of the battle brotherhood. Indeed, *Cross of Iron* is one of Peckinpah's finest studies of the purging of hatred through violence.

Cross of Iron's prologue, particularly when viewed in the overall context of Peckinpah's work, makes clear that there are links between the patriarchy of the Western and the Nazism of Germany even if the origins of the two ideologies differ. This prologue is composed mainly of newsreel footage from the Second World War. Footage used as a recurrent motif shows a troop of youths from the *Hitlerjugend* scaling cliffs with a Nazi flag, finally raising the flag in salute to a mountain face before them. It is understandable Peckinpah should choose to emphasise this salute to the mountain: he did, after all, use infertile landscape to evoke the harshness of patriarchal frontier society in *Pat Garrett*. The mountain imagery is also resonant of American cinema in general: in Anthony Mann's Westerns a barren and formidable landscape is the usual terrain of the revenge quest; while for a number of Walsh heroes mountains are places of brutal nemesis.

Most of *Cross of Iron*'s prologue seeks to link Nazism with the brutality and harshness of a father authority. The continual linking of Hitler with impressionable children introduces Peckinpah's perennial preoccupation with the betrayal of childhood innocence; and, by showing women in the presence of Hitler or SS-officers and then phasing in scenes of warfare, Peckinpah makes his equally familiar link between the need to define an identity through violence and the misogyny that can spring from rivalry with a father authority.

The prologue closes with the spectacle of an exploding shell. Explosions causing random slaughter punctuate the whole movie; and these do not merely show the gratuitous brutality of war, but also seem like the ministrations of some terrible Jehovah. Here again is Peckinpah's recurrent – and characteristically American – equation of Old Testament protestantism with the nightmare aspects of modern technology. Like the American pioneers who went forth to subjugate nature in the name of a puritan authority, the German soldiers on the Russian Front in *Cross of Iron* secretly live in fear of a final punishment for their hubris. 'I have a feeling that one of these days this land will swallow us up', says Colonel Brandt early in the movie; and, during a major Russian offensive, Captain Stransky falls prey to a fear of being swallowed by the turmoil of battle.

Both Brandt and Stransky, rational and charismatic authoritarians respectively, seem degenerate. Brandt's sessions of self-questioning with Captain Kiesel, his ineffectual adjutant, always prove inconclusive; and, for all his concern about a new Germany, Brandt reveals himself to be firmly tied to the old, finally going forth in search of a Wagnerian death with the remnants of his troops. Brandt's faith in the rule-book is shown to be absurd when he seeks to have Stransky reprimanded for making a false claim for an Iron Cross. With dissolves, Peckinpah moves from an investigative Brandt to a corpse in a bloodied stream, then to Stransky arranging the elimination of Steiner for refusing to corroborate his claim for a medal – the same river of blood, it is clear, flows from Brandt as from Stransky; through his toying with army regulations, Brandt merely decorates with respectability a situation that is totally rotten.

When Stransky first arrives at company HQ, he is shown slyly urinating, much to the consternation of an adjutant; and later, flung into mud by the force of an explosion, he writhes there as if in disgust at his own faeces. Here Peckinpah attacks the hygienic images with which aristocracy and monarchy alike endorse cultural repression.

Stransky sees his own identity solely in terms of the class system. Not a Nazi, he feels he has a right to power over others because he is a Prussian aristocrat. He claims that 'a man's true destiny' lies above any complications posed by women and children, that it is 'to be free, to rule, and to fight'. Many of his lines on this subject are taken almost directly from *The Willing Flesh*, the distinguished novel by Willi Heinrich on which the movie is based. Yet what they express is central to Peckinpah's concerns: the confusion of freedom with the will to power is something the director has continually exposed as symptomatic of the American cinema, at times – as at the end of *Straw Dogs* – even embracing this confusion himself with the fury of an injured spirit.

Stransky dotes on his reflection in mirrors, and along with his fear of being swallowed in battle goes a fear of being disfigured during it. It is as he looks in a mirror that Stransky catches a glimpse of Lieutenant Triebig caressing the cheek of Kepler, the latter's adjutant. Here Maximilian Schell's study in controlled hysteria reaches perhaps its greatest height as Stransky insinuatingly forces Triebig and Kepler to acknowledge their homosexuality. When Stransky tells them they will be hung if found out by military authorities, he is also suppressing a homosexuality in himself.

Stransky is Peckinpah's most extreme study in narcissism. Steve Judd, Major Dundee, Pike Bishop, Pat Garrett – all seek by embodying a kind of authority to mould others in the image of a self-love, but ultimately they are forced to reassess in some way the demands of such a love. But Stransky has no capacity for such reassessment: he is a man who wakes up every morning to be greeted by the world in an image of his authority.

Like Pat Garrett earlier, the character of Rolf Steiner provides James Coburn with the opportunity for an impressive study of frustrated integrity. Through Steiner, Peckinpah shows how a man cannot hope to liberate himself by merely hating authority. Steiner claims to reject totally the system he is in. He is dismissive of his promotion to sergeant and treats being decorated with an Iron Cross as a sick joke: he knows that placing a prestige on survival and coming out on top is the way the *status quo* can maintain oppression. Yet this sense of the system's ridiculousness has filled Steiner with such an overpowering hatred that he lives without any faith in life. Steiner's dilemma lends further force to Peckinpah's invective against the military hierarchy. Here the director shows how men like Brandt and Stransky are to be rejected not just for what they represent in themselves but for their capacity to create a world about them that thrives on hatred.

Steiner also appears prey to a similar narcissism to Stransky. In the movie's opening sequence, for instance, Steiner's men efficiently butcher Russians, merely ciphers to his orders. Yet the platoon reject the false values of the officer class. They joke over the discomforts of life in the trenches; and through this openness they contrast both with Stransky in his sly urination, and Kiesel, who whines about his diarrhoea.

It is made clear early in the movie that Steiner's relationship with his platoon is opposite to his with Stransky. Absent-mindedly succumbing to army discipline, Kern, a member of Steiner's platoon, pulls himself to attention before the sergeant; but then he breaks into a smile, army discipline giving way to a feeling of complete equality between two men. From this touching moment, Peckinpah cuts to Steiner standing to attention before Stransky, Stransky's cold stare fuelling the hatred in Steiner.

Steiner's narcissism is underlined by his encounter with the Russian boy soldier whom he and his men take captive when we first see them in action. Seeking to return the child unharmed to the Russians, Steiner apologizes to him for the state of the world as being 'an accident of hands, mine, others – all without mind'. What Steiner is really engaged in here is a dialogue with self where he refuses to take responsibility for his own actions and those of others around him.

In many American movies, notably the Westerns of Hawks and Mann, the taking up of guns and their reloading is a *motif* for the renewal of phallic aggression. Peckinpah uses this *motif* considerably in *Cross of Iron*, particularly in relation to Steiner, who is often seen casting a spent cartridge only to re-insert another immediately into his gun. Before he leaves Steiner in no-man's-land, the child casts him the mouth-organ which, when first captured, he played to spellbind the platoon in a harmonious mood. The gesture visually parallels Steiner's casting away of cartridge cases. It is, perhaps, the child's way of saying that, despite the unnatural terror instilled in Steiner by the army and Stransky, he must not seek to define an identity through aggression, for this can only lead to an inhuman isolation.

The child is killed by attacking Russian troops; and to Steiner the sight of this comes as the execution of some dreadful punishment upon himself. In his demented reaction to the death, Steiner recalls many of Peckinpah's previous heroes: Major Dundee and Pike Bishop in their respective woundings, Cable Hogue confronted with the blasting of the lizard, or Bennie after Elita's death.

It is impossible not to admire Peckinpah's use of the child, who succinctly exteriorizes Steiner's psychodrama. The betrayal of a childhood innocence leading to phallic aggression is a motif of the American cinema that Peckinpah has made his own. Here he uses it to call into question a narcissistic paternalism American cinema has so often celebrated, particularly as a way it should define its position in the world. For instance, *The Green Berets*, John Wayne's Vietnam war movie, ends as platoon leader Wayne takes custody of an orphaned Vietnamese boy whom he calls a symbol of what the war is really about. More complexly, Sam Fuller's *Underworld USA* uses the murder of a little child as one justification for a demonstration of red-blooded right-wing anarchism.

The child in *Cross of Iron* only has a nightmare dimension for Steiner. There is a mysterious – and even angelic – androgyny about him and thus he seems to reintroduce female qualities into a harsh masculine world hostile to them. Taking it upon himself to look after Steiner, he shows a humility that is completely alien to the world of officers and men. At a number of points Peckinpah implies a link between the boy and one or other of Steiner's men. It is after Kern has pointed out a mutilated corpse to Steiner that the child first appears. For his first meeting with Stransky, Steiner is accompanied by the child and Schnurrbart. When Stransky orders Steiner to have the child shot,

Steiner tells him to order the child shot himself, thereby inviting Stransky to become a target for his vengeance. But Schnurrbart takes advantage of an explosion to lead the child away, saving his leader from spiralling into complete hatred.

The humility of the child and the emotional generosity of Steiner's platoon combine in the scene involving the platoon's birthday party for Lieutenant Meyer, the only officer who treats them as an equal. A toast to survival is proposed by Private Dietz, a virginal young new recruit. At the toast, Kern is overcome by terror, seeming to see before his eyes an image of his own eventual brutal dying: but Kruger, Kern's comrade, rushes up to him to stifle his intended scream with a kiss. After this faintly comic and yet moving moment, the child lights a candle in ritual tribute to the men's fellowship; then he gives the still distraught Kern a comforting look as Kern looks away to exchange smiles with Steiner.

The death that *Cross of Iron* extols is a purer erotic experience than in Peckinpah's previous work. It is important that Meyer's birthday celebration should be intercut with Stransky's baiting of the homosexuals, for the taboo Stransky places on the expression of sexuality clouds the whole action of the movie. Death is at once a penalty for loving and the provider of a release from tension and pain, a release that – unlike in *The Killer Elite* – can never be possible in the actual world. In *Straw Dogs*, Niles kissing Janet Hedden caused an outburst of aggression; in *Cross of Iron*, the kiss is born whatever the pain. Through a *motif* that makes a caress interchangeable with death, Steiner and his companions are linked together in a steadily unfolding network of communal pain.

After the death of the child, Steiner charges howling with rage to lose himself amid the turmoil of a Russian offensive. When Steiner sees in horror Meyer bayoneted, Kruger springs forth like a wolf from his heart to gun down Meyer's assailant. But then a mysterious cleansing process begins to take place. As the dying Meyer's head is lifted by Dietz like an angel about to implant a soft kiss on the lieutenant's lips, Steiner is hit by shrapnel, images of verdant landscapes flooding into his mind as if the wounding has guaranteed him entry into some paradise of nature. Yet this sequence is in unusually cold and subdued colours for a Peckinpah pastoral idyll. This is apt, for the dream finally becomes a revelation of Steiner's inability to overcome his fears. Steiner sees himself abandoned in a stream by the child; and the child, his face alien and hostile, rushes to the edge of the stream to hurl again the mouth-organ to Steiner. Steiner, left inconsolable, is joined in the stream by the nurse who, as he lies semi-conscious in hospital during his dreaming, is seen aggressively shining a probing light into his eyes.

Eva, the nurse, consents to become Steiner's mistress. But Steiner can never feel at one with her. He falls prey to a similar fear of disfigurement as Stransky, being haunted by the scarred face of a fellow patient whom at first he has taken for Kruger. He increasingly needs to be with his men; he imagines an apparition of Schnurrbart as well as one of Kruger. Yet what he experiences is not a healthy need for comradeship but an upsurge in his impulse towards narcissism. For him, the image of the child has become deflected onto that of his men. Thus, his return to his platoon comes as a renewal of the narcissistic state he knew before the death of the child. So much is underlined by the fact that Steiner's platoon now has a new member, the showily groomed Zoll, an SS spy.

During his final meeting with Eva, Steiner does not even notice her body as she dresses, so obsessed is he by the idea of returning to war. As they say their last good-byes, Eva faces a photograph of a Nazi officer above a bowl of flowers. If the photograph suggests Steiner's narcissism, it also represents the sinister father figure whom, like so many of Peckinpah's heroes, Steiner unconsciously feels bars him from women and on whom he needs to be revenged.

Steiner can cut himself off from Eva's love, but he never fully manages to set up a barrier against the fellowship of his men; and when, due to Stransky's machinations, his platoon is left behind as the rest of the company retreat, it is their fellowship which breaks down his coldness and makes him abandon his revenge hatred. Through this fellowship, Steiner is finally able to take his place on the rubbish-heap of history with his head held high, knowing there can be no shame in a mediocre destiny in a society that sets more value on titles and false prestige than human life.

In *Cross of Iron*, Peckinpah again is less interested in the initial explosion of a psychopathic anger than in its dying falls. Like *The Killer Elite*, the movie differs from his earlier movies, since it ends not with one but a series of head-on confrontations with the anguish tormenting the hero. Bennie and Pike Bishop each fought his way to some altar of absolute power, and only after the pleasure of desecrating this altar could they renounce the power that came from it. But Steiner, like Mike Locken in *The Killer Elite*, travels far beyond a symbolic act of father-murder, finally arriving at a pain threshhold just to stand there.

Women in Peckinpah's movies are often casualties of the male drive for power: Bennie leads Elita to her death by challenging El Jefe's men; while the Wild Bunch butcher women to demonstrate a phallic authority. In *Cross of Iron*, however, the penalty for such aggression against women is fully paid as, returning to their own lines, Steiner and his men live out an Oedipal homecoming. On entry to a farm, Steiner's platoon murder Russian guards, only to be greeted by Russian women soldiers behaving like a vipers' nest of vengeful mothers. Here the vagina appears not just to be infected as in *The Killer Elite*, but to have teeth. This sequence – like that of Steiner's loss of the child – carries resonances of the dilemma of American identity. In particular, it confronts a sexual guilt that underlies the rootlessness of the Western hero, a guilt whose covert cinematic ancestry goes back at least as far as *Tol'able David*.

Perhaps the only thing by an American director to approach this sequence in remorseless honesty is that of the nymphomaniac ward in Sam Fuller's *Shock Corridor*, but there women are finally prevented from taking vengeance.

In the farmhouse, Steiner shows signs of rejecting the yearning for phallic aggression: he is disturbed by the sight of a bloodied woman dying from a wound; and when the sunken-eyed Anselm, the most bizarre member of the platoon, irrationally attacks one of the women, he pulls him away from her. Kern's first action at the farm is to climb into a tub where one of the women is bathing. Steiner feels compelled to put an end to Kern's playfulness, and he pulls him from the tub. But then the sergeant lingers near the tub, looking cautiously at the woman. He seems to perceive in her nakedness an essential beauty, a beauty to which in Eva he was blind.

Dietz' humility is stressed in earlier scenes. He remains placid during the tank attack; he is also the only one in the platoon to show a regard for nature. In one scene, he plays a game of not treading on beams of light that fall through forest trees. He avoids the beams, he says, since it is supposed to be good luck. If Dietz' behaviour here meets only with a look of rage from Steiner, it is ultimately this humility that helps Steiner come to terms with the cruel happenings at the farm.

In the farmhouse, one of the women persuades Dietz to let her embrace him, knifing him as he succumbs. It is as if the tormented spirit of Angel in *The Wild Bunch* is finally put to rest. Whereas in Teresa's look to Angel as she went to Mapache, it was impossible to discern the full extent of her love, the woman who murders Dietz seems to do so with compassion. At first Steiner is confirmed in his view of life ('I believe God is a sadist and he probably doesn't even know it'), but his heart is mellowed by the dying Dietz' heart-felt plea that the woman with the knife be spared.

Just before entering the farm, Zoll plucks a piece of vegetation to decorate himself. Through this act, he is aptly linked with the Nazi above the flowers in Eva's room. At the farm, he becomes magnetically attracted to a blonde woman, who is led down from the loft by Kruger as if she were some prize. Intercut with Dietz' surrender to the woman with a knife is Zoll's attempt at fellatio with the woman, an incident that recalls Ollinger's ramming of a shotgun in Billy the Kid's chest in *Pat Garrett*. Huddled in a corner of the same barn is a woman in labour, all of which adds to the nightmarishness of the scene, procreation made to seem but the demonstration of an arrogant male authority.

A howl of pain draws Steiner away from Dietz, to find Zoll with his penis bitten off and the subject of Zoll's lust with her head smashed in. Yet he leaves Zoll to the women to kill. It is the beginning of Steiner's rejection of what the army is trying to make of him. In his abandonment of Zoll, he shows himself ready to accept a punishment that became his due when he stole from Eva's bed to choose war as his mistress.

After the platoon have again returned to the forests, Steiner displays for the first time the child's mouth-organ. Maag, the platoon cook, takes it from him to begin a tune; and, listening to the music, the platoon are truly united for the first time since Steiner's return to war. It is in this mood that they move on to their own lines to face a machine-gun manned against them under Triebig's supervision and at Stransky's request.

Steiner's platoon has a vitality that finally manifests itself as something far beyond the mad ecstasy of which Jack London wrote. Where the Wild Bunch need to take up a machine-gun at their end, Steiner's platoon can advance upon one, braving its fire: the ecstasy they experience is a serene one, for it comes from an acceptance of pain as a price of existence.

Schnurrbart is the first to die in the advance upon the machine-gun, having insisted on replacing Steiner at the head. His death comes as a transfigured version of sacrificial scenes elsewhere in Peckinpah's work, like Tyreen's suicide charge or Miller's last stand. For there is no mad assertion of the imperatives of the self in his gesture, just a resignation to bear the price of a platoon's advance.

In the opening of the movie, Maag takes a gun from a dead Russian to shoot at and explode a grenade hurled at the Russian post. But in his death he redeems the callousness of this action. A slow motion shot suspends the moment where Maag catches a gun hurled into the air by Kern in wounded writhing. At first Maag holds the gun above his head as a sign to those at the machine-gun that the platoon do not come as enemies. But the machine-gun continues to fire, bullets fed remorselessly into its chamber. Incensed, Maag uses Kern's gun to return its fire, his own fire becoming less and less as wound after wound is inflected on him. He comes to stand before the machine-gun, it seems, neither in the name of any God in heaven nor of any nation on earth: at his finish, not even in the cause of avenging harm done to the platoon. He stands there merely as a man asking and expecting no quarter.

Like the child's humility, Maag's death poses a different challenge to the thunder of war than the arrogance of Stransky. In the heroism of his dying, he shows the grandeur of individual free-will and he defines this free-will as something separate to the untrammelled will to power of which Stransky fantasized. Even if God is a sadist, this cannot, it is clear, lessen the value of an individual's life; for Maag has all the glory of Job as he bore the plagues of a cruel Jehovah.

The platoon is linked in other ways to the child during this sequence. They have at their last an implicit androgyny about them, since a number of them wear as disguises uniforms taken from the Russian women. There is also a female element to the death of Kern, Peckinpah's use of slow motion again suggestive of sexual surrender. As in the defloration of Dietz, the image of the virgin accepting impregnation emerges from behind that of the weapon-bearing warrior.

The massacre of the platoon heralds the final upswing and fall of aggression in Steiner, who is left howling in no-man's-land as he did before at the death of the child. When Steiner finally confronts Triebig, the faces of the platoon flood into the sergeant's mind, and he fires on the lieutenant in a cold-blooded rage. As Steiner's fire stops, Kruger leaps at Triebig's corpse to hack away at it with a bayonet. Yet if he again plays the wolf from Steiner's heart, this time Kruger's aggression is not so mindless since it is turned on the man who gives him orders, something that often signifies a movement towards enlightenment in Peckinpah's work.

Again placing private malice above his feeling for his men, Steiner takes leave of Kruger and Anselm, the only surviving members of his platoon. But when, having journeyed across a terrain of war and death, he finally reaches Stransky, his attitude has changed. As he stands before Stransky, Steiner shows a heroism similar to Maag before the machine-gun. He just insults Stransky man to man and not in the name of any form of authority. 'Aristocratic pile of Prussian pig shit', Steiner shouts, fiinrg his gun above the captain's head to show the emptiness of soldierly authority. When Steiner tells of Triebig's death, Stransky is completely unmoved. But when Stransky maliciously chides him over the loss of the platoon, tears well up in Steiner's eyes. It is as if each of the deaths of his men has left him with a wound, and only now these wounds have begun to bleed freely. His only reaction is to tell Stransky that the captain is now his platoon, thus joining himself as firmly to Stransky as finally was Melville's Ahab to Moby Dick or Peckinpah's own Bennie to Alfredo's head. In this moment, Steiner sees Stransky less as someone on whom he needs to take revenge than someone from whom he will accept the pain that for him comes with caring, a pain he feared with Eva and for which he paid but vicariously through Zoll. When Steiner first met Stransky and invited him to kill the child, it was in the conviction that the pain would justify a revenge hatred. But now, turning his back on Stransky, he passively invites pain from him in a gesture that recalls Locken's final reaction to Hansen in *The Killer Elite*.

As so often for Peckinpah, morality is something that can only be regenerated out of the twilight reaches of the individual psyche; and while there is a madness about Steiner, this adds to – rather than diminishes – the morality of his final conduct. If for Steiner war is still an addiction, the nature of this addiction has become something liberating. For his need to see 'the crosses of iron grow' is a positive need, one that will teach him that the pain he feels does not give him any lofty prestige. Each new death he sees will mean a new crucifixion for him, a crucifixion he will bear since he knows this links him with the corpses of his platoon strewn across no-man's-land, and with the straw dogs on wastelands throughout the world. If, unlike with Locken in *The Killer Elite*, Steiner's pain does not mellow into a warm desire to meet life, it nevertheless provides him with a way of seeing beyond the loneliness of the avenger.

Finally Steiner leads Stransky away to be swallowed up with him in the chaos of war, the two of them Peckinpah's grimmest addition to the American cinema's fascination with the male duo. Then, in what can only be described as a mystical visitation, the child reappears to fire on Stransky. This, too, has the quality of transfiguration when considered in relation to Peckinpah's other work. Whereas at the end of *The Wild Bunch* the little boy who admired Mapache fired on Pike Bishop in muddled disillusionment, and at the end of *Alfredo Garcia* a little boy confusedly picked up a gun from amid the carnage of El Jefe's house, the child in *Cross of Iron* directly strikes out against the image of a poisonous authority.

At the child's fire, Stransky stumbles. 'How do I reload?' he says, taking over the movie's reloading *motif*. A series of slides of child victims from various wars ends the movie, and the clicking of a slide-projector that accompanies the appearance of each slide is noticeably similar to the sound of a gun being reloaded. Thus, Stransky's question is in a way answered: there is no need for such a reloading since each time an individual subscribes, he endorses a world where Saturn heartlessly devours children.

A note of optimism comes from Steiner. He is heard emitting a bitter laughter. It is a laughter that directly recalls that which accompanies the loss of the gold (and of a destructive authority) at the end of *The Treasure of the Sierra Madre*, much loved by Peckinpah; and thus, despite its bitterness, it is a good laughter since it signals the renunciation of power.

If Steiner is unable to be the harbinger of a free society, he goes out hoping that the repressive society that produced him will end with him. Just as Schnurrbart did for him, he tries to offer to the world that will come after him life on unconditional terms. He does not ask for the imprint of his ego on posterity, nor the continuance of any of those traditions through which the state deludes an individual this can be achieved. If Steiner at his finish stands for anything, it is for a society where an individual is no longer called upon to stifle his inner vitality and murder his capacity to care for anything.

In Peckinpah's other major studies of male groups, *Major Dundee* and *The Wild Bunch*, the members of the groups find only brief moments of true unity; but the veterans of *Cross of Iron* go out together in a convulsion of shared pain. And out of it all Steiner is born again. For although he lives in a society where just to exist means to draw the blood of others, he fights against himself and what that society has made of him to take responsibility for every step he takes. Thus, *Cross of Iron* continues the reaching out beyond an individual anguish in Peckinpah's work.

POSTSCRIPT: CONVOY

Director: Sam Peckinpah; producer: Robert M. Sherman; 2nd unit directors: Walter Kelley, James Coburn; scriptwriter: B. W. L. Norton; chief editor: Graeme Clifford

Despite flaws, *Convoy* shows Peckinpah fairly successfully enlarging upon his preoccupations with cathartic violence. Unlike Major Dundee or Pike Bishop, Rubber Duck refuses to lead a mob of men on a desperate collision course; through a solitary purging of a personal hatred, he discovers a true feeling of equality with the disenchanted truckers who choose him as convoy leader. Like Capra in *Meet John Doe*, Peckinpah seems to think that, should the government fail to serve as the voice of the people, the people will be ready to support any demagogue who opposes the government; yet he progresses beyond such essentially populist assumptions to articulate a view of social relationships that is in no way crudely authoritarian.

Rubber Duck is not without the emotional instability of earlier Peckinpah heroes. On their first meeting Melissa, a photographer, snaps him in a way that implies her humiliation of him; and the Duck's joke comment to a policeman about Melissa wearing nothing under her dress suggests fears about sexual difference. Similar fears cloud the Duck's relationship to the leggy Violet, a waitress. When he tries to make love to her in his truck, he is called away before he has time to see her fully naked; Widow Woman, an Amazonian Negress trucker, radios him that Lyle Wallace, a policeman he hates more than any other, is stirring up trouble in the truckers' diner. Wallace is already disliked by the truckers for demanding bribes to give them unharassed passage; and when he insults Spider Mike, the black trucker lashes out to knock him senseless, Rubber Duck and other truckers beating up two policemen who come to Wallace's aid. Then, bidding farewell to Violet (in a scene full of sexual nostalgia), Rubber Duck sets off in flight with the truckers.

Despite its hero's wariness to them, the women in *Convoy* conspire towards his salvation. When, hitching a ride, Melissa leaves with the Duck in the convoy, the feeling is not one of rivalry between her and Violet but of a mutual acknowledgement of custodianship of the hero. Like the androgynous child in *Cross of Iron*, Melissa - with close-cropped hair and wearing mostly boyish clothes - is a transfigured version of the Western sidekick. If by her boyishness she facilitates the Duck's narcissistic denial of his sexual fears, her gradual absorption among the truckers suggests his transcendence of isolation. Like Melissa, Widow Woman also proves only ostensibly a threat to the hero. In the diner brawl she assumes a protective function towards the Duck, turning her aggression on a policeman; and as the film progresses, she is absorbed into the convoy on terms of mutual dependence.

An important phase in the Duck's moral development begins when, his love-making again disturbed, he is called away from Melissa by the business of running the convoy. He then goes on to meet Haskins, a politician, who, impressed by the convoy's power, is trying to win votes by showing the truckers sympathy. The Duck rejects Haskins' blandishments, rushing away to the aid of Spider Mike, whom he learns is in gaol and being beaten by the police. The breaking of Spider Mike is a necessary parallel to the Duck's flirtation with omnipotence at the head of the convoy, suggesting the terror of humiliation driving the Duck to prove himself through power. Rescuing Mike, the Duck finds it was not Wallace but another policeman who did the beating; thus he comes to see beyond his hatred of Wallace, reaching a more widespread understanding of a society corrupted by power. The Duck also experiences a sense of obligation to Mike for having undergone a humiliation he himself felt was his due; and at this recognition of mutual dependence he is reunited with Melissa and the truckers, who out of their own free will come to help him in the freeing of Spider Mike.

In contrast to the Wild Bunch or Major Dundee's troop, the convoy does not seek aggression as the ultimate means of defining an identity, the majority of truckers finally halted when they avoid running down children. Rubber Duck also comes to conform to such a definition of identity, Peckinpah asserting - as in much of his later work - that the really important thing is not to bring down the system, but to murder the fascist in oneself. Shortly after the convoy first takes to the road, the Duck disperses a police road-block by recklessly charging it with his truck which is carrying explosives. Here the Duck seems as fascistic as the police about him, Peckinpah focussing repeatedly on his hero's crazed eyes to suggest an absence of concern both for Melissa - who is also in the truck - and over whatever destruction may result. Yet when, irrevocably cut off from the convoy at the close of the movie, the Duck charges a National Guard barricade, he has freed himself from his thirst for power. He puts Melissa down before advancing, then he dons dark glasses, the gesture implying some Oedipal blinding to be contingent upon his parting from Melissa. As the Duck drives on a machine-gun manned by Wallace, we are close to the sacrificial death of Maag in *Cross of Iron:* existence is shown to derive meaning when a man goes on asking no quarter, asserting a claim to individuality in the face of a full awareness of his mortality and vulnerability.

The film ends with Melissa - now dressed in more recognizably female clothes - reunited with the Duck, who has escaped the destruction of his truck, and who - seemingly ready to shed his butch identity - answers to his original name of Martin Penwald. Yet if this symbolism suggests the Duck no longer fears vulnerability in himself and femaleness in general, Kris Kristofferson's performance has hardly indicated an evolution to love and trusting. Badly acted and underwritten, Ali McGraw's Melissa also lets down the film's attempt to go beyond butch relationships to heterosexual union. Melissa is never fully a character in her own right, seeming to change identities mechanically in accordance with how the Duck sees her. The most convincing features about the end of the movie are the resolutions of the Duck's relationships to Lyle and to the truckers. Discovering the Duck's survival, the lawman turns a blind eye. He too has transcended hatred, presumably now understanding that the sickness lies in the hierarchical nature of the system, and no longer contemptuous of the truckers or their unionizing. If the Duck's advance on the machine-gun teaches Wallace the importance of respecting another's right to liberty, it gives to the truckers a special pride in their own individuality. At the close of the movie the convoy move off in a gesture of disgust at Haskins' funeral oration for its supposedly dead leader. Since neither the Duck nor any other leader is at the convoy's head, it seems that each of its members is at last able to take responsibility for his actions - Peckinpah's concept of an ideal society.

FILMOGRAPHY

Sam Peckinpah was born in 1926 in Southern California. His family history is bound up with pioneer times. He had a grandmother who was a Paiute Indian and a grandfather who bought himself a mountain and built a saw-mill on it. Like this grandfather, Peckinpah's father and brothers all became Superior Court Judges. 'When I was a kid I grew up with those people sitting around with my uncle. Sitting around a dining room table talking about law and order, truth and justice, on a Bible which was very big in our family. I suppose I felt like an outsider, and I started to question them. I guess I'm still questioning.'

Peckinpah studied law briefly. He also spent four years in the Marines and fought against the Japanese in China. 'I fell in love with a Chinese girl; I wanted to marry her and stay . . . I first began my studies of Zen in China.' In the Marines, Peckinpah came to know men who lived solely for violence.

After taking an M.A. in Drama at the University of Southern California, Peckinpah worked for several years in the theatre as an actor and director. For reasons which were 'mostly economic' he then took a job with KLAC-TV as a stage-hand. This job came to an end when Peckinpah was fired from a show of Liberace's for not wearing a suit.

Next Peckinpah took a job as dialogue director to Don Siegel. Peckinpah has a great deal of affection for Siegel but claims Siegel stole *Hound Dog Man* from him, which he considers to be Siegel's best film. On Siegel's *Invasion of The Body Snatchers* Peckinpah played some dozen of the minor characters and also did a rewrite of the script – with its fugitive lovers in an unfeeling world, *Invasion of The Body Snatchers* seems something of a precursor of *The Getaway*. Following his association with Siegel, Peckinpah worked on a number of small budget movies; he appears briefly as a bank clerk in Jacques Tourneur's *Wichita*.

Peckinpah began writing scripts for television and worked on a number of other television series, including *Klondike, Broken Arrow* and *Rifleman*. In television Peckinpah worked with Charles Marquis Warren, director of a number of excellent Westerns including *Arrowhead* and scriptwriter of *The Day of the Evil Gun*. At NBC Dick Powell gave Peckinpah the chance to produce a television series of his own – *The Westerner*. 'Don Siegel really got me started and taught me the basic steps of how to work . . . but it was Dick Powell who gave me the chance to direct, produce and gave me total freedom'. After *Ride the High Country*, Peckinpah directed two shows for *The Dick Powell Theatre – Pericles on 34th Street* and *The Losers*. In the last of these he experimented with speeded-up motion.

Over the years Peckinpah has built up a stock company out of actors like L.Q. Jones and Strother Martin. Peckinpah's favourite cameraman has been Lucien Ballard. Ballard is a master at shooting in twilight as the close of *The Wild Bunch* shows. Peckinpah has also worked memorably with John Coquillon; the nocturnal climaxes of *Straw Dogs* and *Pat Garrett and Billy the Kid* owe much of their atmosphere to Coquillon's ingenuity. Peckinpah claims that Frank Santillo, with whom he first worked on *Ride the High Country*, helped him most in developing editing techniques for action sequences. Jerry Fielding has been the director's most regular composer.

Apart from Ford and Huston, Peckinpah claims to admire Kurosawa, Delmer Daves (particularly *The Hanging Tree* and *Jubal), Billy Wilder (Ace in the Hole)* and René Clement *(Forbidden Games)*. Writers whose influences he claims are Sartre, Cela *(La Familia de Pascual Duarte)*, Carlos Fuentes *(The Death Of Artemio Cruz)*, Heller *(Catch 22)*, Hemingway *(The Old Man and the Sea)*, Faulkner, John MacDonald, Ernest Haycox, Theodore Lipps and Ray Bradbury.

So far unrealized projects include: *The Hi-Lo Country*, a Western novel by Max Evans; *Ready for the Tiger*, a study of children corrupting adults; a film about Panco Villa; Ray Bradbury's *Something Wicked This Way Comes;* and a musical set in Mexico.

The Deadly Companions (1961)

Production Company	Pathé-America-Carousel
Producer	Charles B.FitzSimons

Director	Sam Peckinpah
Script	A.S.Fleischman, based on his own novel
Director of Photography	William H.Clothier (filmed in Panavision)
Colour Process	Pathé Color
Editor	Stanley E.Rabjon
Music	Marlin Skiles
Sound	Robert J.Callen

Maureen O'Hara (Kit Tilden), Brian Keith (Yellowleg), Steve Cochran (Billy), Chill Wills (Turk), Strother Martin (Parson), Will Wright (Doctor), Jim O'Hara (Cal), Peter O'Crotty (Mayor), Billy Vaughan (Mead), Robert Sheldon (Gambler), John Hamilton (Gambler), Hank Gobble (Bartender), Buck Sharpe (Indian).
Running time: 79 mins. Original running time: 90 mins.
Distributor: Columbia-Warner.
First shown in Britain in 1962.

Among its many setbacks, this film was almost ruined by the colour laboratory that processed it. Consequently, no such thing exists as a decent print of the film.

Incidentally, the brilliant use of long shot for the appearance of the Indian-manned stagecoach was the result of a tight schedule – Peckinpah found he had no time to set up close-ups.

Ride the High Country (1961)

Production Company	MGM
Producer	Richard E.Lyons
Director	Sam Peckinpah
Assistant Director	Hal Polaire
Script	N.B.Stone, Jnr
Director of Photography	Lucien Ballard (filmed in CinemaScope)
Colour Process	Metrocolor
Editor	Frank Santillo
Art Directors	George W.Davis, Leroy Coleman
Set Decoration	Henry Grace, Otto Siegal
Music	George Bassman
Sound	Franklin Milton

Randolph Scott (Gil Westrum), Joel McCrea (Steve Judd), Ronald Starr (Heck Longtree), Mariette Hartley (Elsa Knudsen), James Drury (Billy Hammond), R.G.Armstrong (Joshua Knudsen), Edgar Buchanan (Judge Tolliver), Jenie Jackson (Kate), John Anderson (Elder Hammond), L.Q.Jones (Sylvus Hammond), Warren Oates (Henry Hammond), John Davis Chandler (Jimmy Hammond), Carmen Philips (Saloon Girl).
Running time: 93 mins.
Distributor: MGM.
British title: *Guns in the Afternoon.*
First shown in Britain in 1962.

'The film was made in three or four weeks. It was released as part of a double bill in the USA and it was the British and French critics who discovered it and forced its recognition in the USA, making the critics there reconsider their judgement . . . or absence of judgement of it. That is why I can say to journalists today that they bear the responsibility for my films, for *The Wild Bunch*, which I could not have made without their support, particularly after *Major Dundee*.'

Major Dundee (1964)

Production Company	Jerry Bresler Productions
Producer	Jerry Bresler
Director	Sam Peckinpah
Assistant Directors	Floyd Joyer, John Veitch
Second Unit Director	Cliff Lyons
Script	Harry Julian Fink, Oscar Saul, Sam Peckinpah from a story by Harry Julian Fink
Director of Photography	Sam Leavitt (filmed in Panavision)
Colour Process	Eastman Colour by Pathé. Print by Technicolor
Editors	William Lyon, Don Starling, Howard Kunin
Art Director	Al Ybarra
Special Effects	August Lohman
Music	Daniele Amfitheatrof

Title song	Daniele Amfitheatrof, Ned Washington
Sung by	Mitch Miller's Sing Along Gang
Costumes	Tom Dawson
Sound	Charles J.Rice, James Z.Flaster

Charlton Heston (Major Amos Dundee), Richard Harris (Captain Benjamin Tyreen), Jim Hutton (Lt Graham), James Coburn (Samuel Potts), Michael Anderson Jnr (Tim Ryan), Senta Berger (Teresa Santiago), Mario Adorf (Sgt Gomez), Brock Peters (Aesop), Warren Oates(O.W. Hadley), Ben Johnson (Sgt Chillum), R.G.Armstrong (Revd Dahlstrom), L.Q. Jones (Arthur Hadley), Slim Pickens (Wiley), Karl Swenson (Capt. Waller), Michael Pate (Sierra Charriba), John Davis Chandler (Jimmy Lee Benteen), Dub Taylor (Priam), Albert Carriere (Capt. Jacques Tremaine), José Carlos Ruiz (Riago), Aurora Clavell (Melinche), Begonia Palacios (Linda), Enrique Lucero (Doctor Aguilar), Francisco Reyguera (Old Apache).
Running time: 120 mins. Original running time: 134 mins.
Distributor: Columbia-Warner.
First shown in Britain in 1965.

A list of many of the scenes cut from this film exists in Jim Kitses' *Horizons West*. Peckinpah claims that many of these scenes contained his first experiments with slow-motion violence.

Following *Major Dundee*, Peckinpah began directing *The Cincinnati Kid* which starred Steve McQueen, but after a few days he was replaced by Norman Jewison. Unable to secure further work as a director he turned to writing scripts: besides *The Glory Guys* (1966), he worked with Robert Towne on the script for Buzz Kulick's *Villa Rides!* (1968). During this time, Peckinpah also returned to television to direct a highly successful version of Katherine Anne Porter's *Noon Wine*.

The Wild Bunch (1969)

Production Company	Warner Brothers Seven Arts
Producer	Phil Feldman
Director	Sam Peckinpah
2nd Unit Director	Buzz Henry
Assistant Directors	Cliff Coleman, Fred Gamon
Screenplay	Walon Green and Sam Peckinpah, from a story by Walon Green and Roy N. Sickner
Director of Photography	Lucien Ballard
Colour Process	Technicolor
Editor	Louis Lombardo
Art Director	Edward Garrere
Music	Jerry Fielding

William Holden (Bishop), Ernest Borgnine (Dutch), Robert Ryan (Thornton), Edmond O'Brien (Sykes), Warren Oates (Lyle Gorch), Jaime Sanchez (Angel), Ben Johnson (Tector Gorch), Emilio Fernandez (Mapache), Strother Martin (Coffer), L.Q.Jones (T.C.), Albert Dekker (Harrigan), Bo Hopkins (Crazy Lee), Dub Taylor (Wainscoat), Jorge Russek (Zamorra), Alfonso Arau (Herrera), Chano Urueta (Don José), Sonia Emilio (Teresa), Aurora Clavell (Aurora), Elsa Cardenas (Elsa).
Running time: 145 mins.
Distributor: Columbia-Warner.

The Ballad of Cable Hogue (1969)

Production Company	Warner Brothers
Producer	Sam Peckinpah
Director	Sam Peckinpah
Screenplay	John Crawford, Edmund Penney
Director of Photography	Lucien Ballard
Colour Process	Technicolor
Editors	Frank Santillo, Lou Lombardo
Art Director	Leroy Coleman
Music	Jerry Goldsmith
Songs (sung by Richard Gillis)	'Tomorrow is the song I sing' by Jerry Goldsmith and Richard Gillis; 'Wait for me', 'Sunrise' by Richard Gillis

Jason Robards Jnr (Cable Hogue), Stella Stevens (Hildy), David Warner (Joshua), Strother Martin (Bowen), Slim Pickens

(Ben Fairchild), L.Q.Jones (Taggart), Peter Whitney (Cushing), R.G.Armstrong (Quittner), Gene Evans (Clete), William Mims (Jensen), Kathleen Freeman (Mrs Jensen), Susan O'Connell (Claudia), Vaughn Taylor (Powell), Felix Nelson (William), Max Evans (Web Seely), Darwin W.Lamb (First Customer), James Anderson (Preacher).
Running time: 114 mins.
Distributor: Columbia-Warner.
First shown in Britain in 1971.

This film was unduly cut after Peckinpah finished it. Most notably perhaps, a comic brawl between Robards, Warner and Gene Evans is missing.

Straw Dogs (1970)

Production Company	Talent Associates/ Amerbroco for ABC Pictures
Producer	Daniel Melnick
Director	Sam Peckinpah
Assistant Director	Terry Marcel
Script	David Zelag Goodman, Sam Peckinpah
Director of Photography	John Coquillon
Colour Process	Eastman Colour
Editor	Paul Davies
Art Director	Ken Bridgeman
Music	Jerry Fielding

Dustin Hoffman (David Sumner), Susan George (Amy Sumner), Peter Vaughn (Tom Hedden), T.P.McKenna (Major Scott), Del Henney (Venner), Ken Hutchison (Scutt), Colin Welland (Revd Hood), Jim Norton (Cawsey), Sally Thomsett (Janice), Donald Webster (Riddaway), Len Jones (Bobby Hedden), Peter Arne (John Niles), Robert Keegan (Harry Ware), June Brown (Mrs Hedden), Cloe Franks (Emma Hedden), Cherina Mann (Mrs Hood).
Running time: 118 mins.
Distributor: Fox-Rank.

Junior Bonner (1971)

Production Company	Joe Wizan-Booth Gardner/Solar for ABC Pictures
Producer	Joe Wizan
Director	Sam Peckinpah
2nd Unit Director	Frank Kowalski
Assistant Director	Frank Baur
Script	Jeb Rosebrook
Director of Photography	Lucien Ballard (Todd AO-35)
Colour Process	Movielab
Editor	Robert Wolf
Art Director	Edward S.Howarth
Music	Jerry Fielding
Songs	'Arizona Morning', 'Rodeo Man' written and sung by Rod Hart

Steve McQueen (Junior Bonner), Robert Preston (Ace Bonner), Ida Lupino (Elvira Bonner), Joe Don Baker (Curly Bonner), Charmagne (Barbara Leigh), Mary Murphy (Ruth Bonner), Ben Johnson (Buck Roan), Bill McKinney (Red Terwilliger), Sandra Deel (Nurse Arlis), Donald 'Red' Barry (Homer Rutledge), Dub Taylor (Del), Charles Gray (Burt), Matthew Peckinpah (Tim Bonner), Sundown Spencer (Nick Bonner), Rita Garrison (Flashie).
Running time: 103 mins.
Distributor: Fox-Rank.

This film was actually shot during rodeo time in Prescott, Arizona. Peckinpah used 'six cameras with actual events, made me feel like I was planning an assault on Iwo Jima'.

The Getaway (1972)

Production Company	Solar/First Artists. A Foster-Brower production
Producer	David Foster
Associate Producer	Gordon T.Dawson
2nd Unit Director	Gordon T.Dawson
Director	Sam Peckinpah
Assistant Directors	Newton Arnold, Ron Wright
Script	Walter Hill, based on the novel by Jim Thompson
Director of Photography	Lucien Ballard (Todd-AO)
Colour Process	Technicolor
Editor	Robert Wolfe
Art Directors	Ted Haworth, Angelo Graham

Set Decoration	George R.Nelson
Music	Quincy Jones
Harmonica Solos	Toots Thielmans
Musical Voices	Don Elliott

Steve McQueen (Doc McCoy), Ali McGraw (Carol McCoy), Ben Johnson (Jack Benyon), Sally Struthers (Fran Clinton), Al Lettieri (Rudy Butler), Slim Pickens (Cowboy), Richard Bright (Thief), Jack Dodson (Harold Clinton), Dub Taylor (Laughlin), Bo Hopkins (Frank Jackson), Roy Jenson (Cully), John Bryson (acccountant), Tom Runyon (Swain), Whitney Jones (Soldier), Raymond King & Ivan Thomas (Boys on Train), Brenda W.King & C.W.White (Boys' Mothers), W.Dee Kutach (Parole Board Chairman), Brick Lowry (Parole Board Commissioner), Martin Colley (McCoy's Lawyer), O.S. Savage (Field Captain), A.L.Camp (Hardware Store Owner), Rob Veal (TV Shop Proprietor), Bruce Bissonette (Sporting Goods Salesman), Maggie Gonzalez (Car-Hop), Jim Kannon (Cannon), Doug Dudley (Max), Stacy Newton (Stacy), Tom Bush (Cowboy's Helper).

Running time: 122 mins.
Distributor: Scotia-Barber.
First shown in Britain in 1973.

Pat Garrett and Billy the Kid (1973)

Production Company	MGM
Producer	Gordon Carroll
Director	Sam Peckinpah
2nd Unit Director	Gordon Dawson
Assistant Directors	Newton Arnold, Lawrence J.Powell
Mexican Assistant Director	Jesus Marin Bello
Script	Rudolph Wurlitzer
Director of Photography	John Coquillon (Panavision)
Colour Process	Metrocolor
2nd Unit Photography	Gabriel Torres G.
Editors	Roger Spottiswoode, Garth Craven, Robert L.Woolfe, Richard Halsey, David Berlatsky, Tony de Zarraga
Art Director	Ted Haworth
Set Decoration	Ray Moyer
Music/Songs	Bob Dylan. Sung by Bob Dylan

James Coburn (Pat Garrett), Kris Kristofferson (Billy the Kid), Bob Dylan (Alias), Richard Jaeckel (Sheriff Kip McKinney), Katy Jurado (Mrs Baker), Slim Pickens (Sheriff Baker), Chill Wills (Lemuel), Jason Robards (Governor Lew Wallace), R.G.Armstrong (Deputy Ollinger), Luke Askew (Eno), John Beck (Poe), Richard Bright (Holly), Matt Clark (Deputy J.W.Bell), Rita Coolidge (Maria), Jack Dodson (Howland), Jack Elam (Alamosa Bill), Emilio Fernandez (Paco), Paul Fix (Pete Maxwell), L.Q.Jones (Black Harris), Jorge Russek (Silva), Charlie Martin Smith (Bowdre), Harry Dean Stanton (Luke), Claudia Bryar (Mrs Horrell), John Chandler (Norris), Mike Mikler (Denver), Walter Kelly (Rupert), Rudolph Wurlitzer (Tom O'Folliard), Gene Evans (Horrell), Rutanya Alda (Ruthie Lee), Donnie Fritts (Beaver), Sam Peckinpah (Will). In scenes now cut Barrie Sullavan played Chisum and Aurora Clavell played Garrett's wife.

Running time: 106 mins.
Distributor: MGM/EMI.

Peckinpah regrets the manner studio cuts have changed the meaning of the film: 'This was the story of a time – a legend – not about two gunfighters'.

Bring Me the Head of Alfredo Garcia (1974)

Production Company	Optimus Productions (Hollywood)/ Estudios Churubusco (Mexico City). A Martin Baum-Sam Peckinpah production.
Executive Producer	Helmut Dantine
Producer	Martin Baum
Associate Producer	Gordon Dawson
Director	Sam Peckinpah
Assistant Directors	William C. Davidson, Jesus Marin

Script	Gordon Dawson, Sam Peckinpah
Story	Frank Kowalski, Sam Peckinpah
Director of Photography	Alex Phillips Jnr
Colour Process	DeLuxe
Supervising Editor	Garth Craven
Editors	Robbe Roberts, Sergio Ortega, Dennis E.Dolan
Art Director	Agustin Huarte
Set Decoration	Enrique Estevez
Music	Jerry Fielding
Songs	'Bennie's Song' by and sung by Isela Vega; 'Bad Blood Baby' by Sam Peckinpah; 'A Donde Ir' by Javier Vega, sung by Isela Vega; 'J.F.' by Arturo Castro.

Warren Oates (Bennie), Isela Vega (Elita), Gig Young (Quill), Robert Webber (Sappensly), Helmut Dantine (Max), Emilio Fernandez (El Jefe), Kris Kristofferson (Paco), Donny Fritts (John), Chano Urueta (One-armed Bartender), Jorge Russek (Cueto), Don Levy (Frank), Chalo Gonzalez (Chalo), Enrique Lucero (Estaban), Janine Maldonado (Teresa), Tamara Garina (Grandmother Moreno), Farnesio De Bernal (Bernardo), Ahui Camacho (El Chavito), Monica Miguel (Dolores de Escomiglia), Paco Pharres (Carpenter), Juan Manuel Diaz (Paulo), René Dupeyron (Angel), Yolando Ponce (Yolo), Juan José Palacios (Juan), Manolo (Tourist Guide), Neri Ruiz (Maria), Roberto Dumont (Chavo).
Running time: 112 mins.
Distributor: United Artists.

The Killer Elite (1975)

Production Company	Exeter/Persky-Bright
Executive Producer	Helmut Dantine
Co-Producers	Martin Baum and Arthur Lewis
Director	Sam Peckinpah
Music Composed and Conducted by	Jerry Fielding
Screenplay	Stirling Silliphant
Director of Photography	Phil Lathrop (Panavision)
Colour Process	DeLuxe
1st Assistant Director	Newton Arnold
2nd Assistant Director	Ron Wright and Jim Bloom
1st Assistant Director/2nd Unit	Cliff Coleman
2nd Unit Director/Script Supervisor	Frank Kowalski
Art Director	Ted Haworth
Assistant Art Director	Ron Hobbs
Film Editor	Garth Craven

James Caan (Mike Locken), Robert Duvall (George Hansen), Arthur Hill (Cap Collis), Gig Young (Laurence Weyburn), Mako (Yuen Chung), Bo Hopkins (Miller), Burt Young (Mac), Tom Clancey (O'Leary), Tiana (Tommie Chung), Katy Heflin (Amy), James Wing Woo (Tao Yi), George Kee Cheung (Bruce), Simon Tam (Jimmy Fung), Rick Alemany (Ben Otake), Hank Hamilton (Hank), Walter Kelly (Walter), Billy J.Scott (Eddie), Johnnie Burrell (Donnie), Matthew Peckinpah (Kid), Carole Mallory (Rita), Tommy Bush (Sam), Eddie Donno (Fake Officer), Victor Sen Young (Wei Chi), Wilfred Tsang (Wilgie), Milton Shoong (Milton), Sondra Blake (Josephine), Kim Kahana (Association Guard), Eddie White (Security Policeman), Al Keller (Cop), Mel Cenizal (Waiter), Gary Combs (Security Policeman), James De Closs (Soldier), Joseph D. Glenn (Man at Com-Teg), Eliose Shoong (Eloise), Charles A. Titone (Soldier at party), Kuo Lien Ying (Tai Chi Master), Christy Weston (Weyburn's Secretary), Helmut Dantine ('Vorodny').
Running Time: 123 mins.
Distributor: United Artists.
First shown in Britain in 1976.

Monte Hellman was scheduled to direct *Pat Garrett and Billy the Kid* but the studio lost faith in him with the commercial failure of his *Two-Lane Blacktop*. Presumably Hellman gained a job as an editor on *The Killer Elite* because Peckinpah regretted being put in the position of ousting him from the earlier movie.

Cross of Iron (1977)

Production Company	Anglo-EMI (London)/Rapid Film (Munich) Terra Filmkunst (West Berlin)
Producer	Wolf Hartwig
Director	Sam Peckinpah
Screenplay	Julius J.Epstein and Herbert Asmodi from the book *The Willing Flesh* by Willi Heinrich
Director of Photography	John Coquillon
Colour Process	Technicolour
Editors	Tony Lawson, Mike Ellis
Assistant Director	Bert Batt
Production Designers	Ted Haworth, Brian Ackland Snow
Music	Ernest Gold

James Coburn (Sgt Steiner), Maximilian Schell (Capt. Stransky), James Mason (Col. Brandt), David Warner (Capt. Kiesel), Klaus Lowitsch (Kruger), Roger Fritz (Lt Triebig), Vadim Glowna (Kern), Fred Stillkraut (Schnurrbart), Burkhardt Driest (Maag), Dieter Schidor (Anselm), Michael Nowka (Dietz), Veronique Vendell (Marga), Arthur Brauss (Zoll), Slavco Stimac (the child), Senta Berger (Eva).
Running time: 133 mins.
Distributor: EMI.

It is small wonder that the narrative has a few rough edges, since production money was stopped before shooting in Yugoslavia had been completed. Peckinpah and his crew worked for several weeks without salary to complete shooting. More was to have been shot of the final holocaust. Stransky's final stumble was a consequence of Maximilian Schell tripping up during the shooting of the last reel of film, an accident which, Peckinpah admits, provides a perfect close to the movie. Peckinpah is satisfied with the film as it now stands, claiming post-production work in England made it possible to save it.

BIBLIOGRAPHY

Studies and articles I found useful in terms of cultural background were: Leslie Fiedler's *Love and Death In the American Novel;* Edmund Wilson's *Patriotic Gore;* Henry Nash Smith's *Mark Twain: the Development Of a Writer;* Daniel G. Hoffman's *The Poetry Of Stephen Crane;* 'The White Negro' in Norman Mailer's *Advertisements For Myself;* 'In Nomine Diaboli' by Henry A. Murray in *Melville: Twentieth Century Views* and 'The Blue Hotel: a Psychoanalytic Study' by Daniel Weiss in *Stephen Crane: Twentieth Century Views.*

So far little has appeared on Peckinpah in book form. An interesting study of the director can be found in Jim Kitses' *Horizons West,* and Max Evans' *Sam Peckinpah: Master of Violence* is an anecdotal account of the man and of the making of *The Ballad Of Cable Hogue.*